Get your facts straight with CGP!

This CGP Knowledge Organiser has one mission in life — helping you remember the key facts for Edexcel GCSE Chemistry.

We've boiled every topic down to the vital definitions, facts and diagrams, making it all easy to memorise.

There's also a matching Knowledge Retriever book that'll test you on every page. Perfect for making sure you know it all!

CGP — still the best! ☺

Our sole aim here at CGP is to produce the highest quality books — carefully written, immaculately presented and dangerously close to being funny.

Then we work our socks off to get them out to you — at the cheapest possible prices.

Contents

Working Scientifically
The Scientific Method 2
Designing & Performing Experiments 3
Presenting Data 4
Conclusions, Evaluations and Units 5

Topic 1 — Key Concepts in Chemistry
Chemical Equations 6
Hazards and History of the Atom 7
Atoms, Elements and Isotopes 8
The Periodic Table 9
Electronic Configurations and Ions 10
Ionic Substances and Bonding Models 11
Molecular Substances 12
More Covalent Substances 13
Metallic Bonding, Metals
  & Non-Metals 14
Mass, Moles and Limiting Reactants 15
Concentration and Empirical Formulas 16
Equations and Conservation of Mass 17

Topic 2 — States of Matter and Mixtures
States of Matter 18
Purity 19
Separation Techniques 20
Chromatography 21
Water Treatment 22

Topic 3 — Chemical Changes
Acids and Bases 23
Strong and Weak Acids 24
Insoluble and Soluble Salts 25
Electrolysis 26
More on Electrolysis 27

Topic 4 — Extracting Metals and Equilibria
Reactivity of Metals 28
Extracting Metals 29
Recycling and Life Cycle Assessments 30
Reversible Reactions 31

Topic 5 — Separate Chemistry 1
Metals and Alloys 32
Corrosion 33
Gases and Titrations 34
Percentage Yield and Atom Economy 35
The Haber Process 36
Fertilisers and Fuel Cells 37

Topic 6 — Groups in the Periodic Table
Group 1 and Group 0 Elements 38
Group 7 Elements 39

Topic 7 — Rates of Reaction and Energy Changes
Rates of Reaction 40
Factors Affecting Rates of Reaction 41
Endothermic & Exothermic Reactions 42

Topic 8 — Fuels and Earth Science

Hydrocarbons...43
Fractional Distillation and Cracking..........44
Pollutants and Fuels...................................45
The Atmosphere..46
Greenhouse Gases & Climate Change....47

Topic 9 — Separate Chemistry 2

Tests for Ions..48
More Tests and Flame Photometry.............49
Types of Hydrocarbons...............................50
Addition Polymers.......................................51
More Polymers and Plastics........................52
Alcohols and Carboxylic Acids...................53
Nanoparticles and Materials.......................54

Core Practicals

Core Practicals 1..55
Core Practicals 2..56
Core Practicals 3..57
Core Practicals 4..58
Core Practicals 5..59

Practical Skills

Apparatus and Techniques.............................60
Practical Techniques......................................61
Equipment and Heating Substances..........62

Published by CGP.
From original material by Richard Parsons.

Editors: Emma Clayton, Emily Forsberg, Sarah Pattison and George Wright.
Contributor: Paddy Gannon.

With thanks to Katie Fernandez, Luke Molloy and Jamie Sinclair for the proofreading.
With thanks to Emily Smith for the copyright research.

ISBN: 978 1 78908 848 9

Hazard symbols used on p.7 contain public sector information published by the Health and Safety Executive and licensed under the Open Government Licence. http://www.nationalarchives.gov.uk/doc/open-government-licence/version/3/

Printed by Elanders Ltd, Newcastle upon Tyne.
Clipart from Corel®
Illustrations by: Sandy Gardner Artist, email sandy@sandygardner.co.uk

Text, design, layout and original illustrations © Coordination Group Publications Ltd (CGP) 2022
All rights reserved.

Photocopying more than one section of this book is not permitted, even if you have a CLA licence.
Extra copies are available from CGP with next day delivery. • 0800 1712 712 • www.cgpbooks.co.uk

The Scientific Method

Developing Theories

Come up with hypothesis → Test hypothesis → Evidence is peer-reviewed → If all evidence backs up hypothesis, it becomes an accepted theory.

HYPOTHESIS — a possible explanation for an observation.

PEER REVIEW — when other scientists check results and explanations before they're published.

Accepted theories can still change over time as more evidence is found, e.g. the theory of atomic structure:

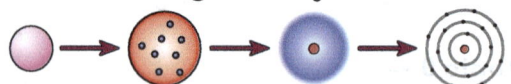

Models

REPRESENTATIONAL MODELS — a simplified description or picture of the real system, e.g. the different ways of showing covalent bonding:

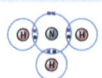 Dot and cross model

 Ball and stick model

Models help scientists explain observations and make predictions.

COMPUTATIONAL MODELS — computers are used to simulate complex processes.

Issues in Science

Scientific developments can create four types of issue:

1. **Economic** — e.g. beneficial technology, like alternative energy sources, may be too expensive to use.
2. **Environmental** — e.g. new technology could harm the natural environment.
3. **Social** — decisions based on research can affect people, e.g. taxes on fossil fuels.
4. **Personal** — some decisions affect individuals, e.g. a person may not want a wind farm being built near to their home.

Media reports on scientific developments may be oversimplified, inaccurate or biased.

Hazard and Risk

HAZARD — something that could potentially cause harm.

RISK — the chance that a hazard will cause harm.

Hazards associated with chemistry experiments include:

 Corrosive chemicals e.g. sulfuric acid

Faulty electrical equipment

Fire from Bunsen burners

The seriousness of the harm and the likelihood of it happening both need consideration.

Designing & Performing Experiments

Collecting Data

	Data should be...	
REPEATABLE	Same person gets same results after repeating experiment using the same method and equipment.	Reliable data is repeatable and reproducible.
REPRODUCIBLE	Similar results can be achieved by someone else, or by using a different method or piece of equipment.	Valid results are repeatable and reproducible and answer the original question.
ACCURATE	Results are close to the true answer.	
PRECISE	All data is close to the mean.	

Fair Tests

INDEPENDENT VARIABLE	Variable that you change.
DEPENDENT VARIABLE	Variable that is measured.
CONTROL VARIABLE	Variable that is kept the same.
CONTROL EXPERIMENT	An experiment kept under the same conditions as the rest of the investigation without anything being done to it.
FAIR TEST	An experiment where only the independent variable changes, whilst all other variables are kept the same.

A fair test

Control experiments are carried out when variables can't be controlled.

Four Things to Look Out For

1. **RANDOM ERRORS** — unpredictable differences caused by things like human errors in measuring.
2. **SYSTEMATIC ERRORS** — measurements that are wrong by the same amount each time.
3. **ZERO ERRORS** — systematic errors that are caused by using a piece of equipment that isn't zeroed properly.
4. **ANOMALOUS RESULTS** — results that don't fit with the rest of the data.

Anomalous results can be ignored if you know what caused them.

Processing Data

Calculate the mean — add together all repeat measurements and divide by number of measurements.

UNCERTAINTY — the amount by which a mean result may differ from the true value.

$$\text{uncertainty} = \frac{\text{range}}{2}$$

largest measurement minus smallest measurement

In any calculation, you should round the answer to the lowest number of significant figures (s.f.) given.

Working Scientifically

Presenting Data

Bar Charts

Bar charts can be used when independent variable is categoric or discrete.

- linear scale
- units
- labelled axes
- bars same width

Discrete data can only take certain values with no in-between values.

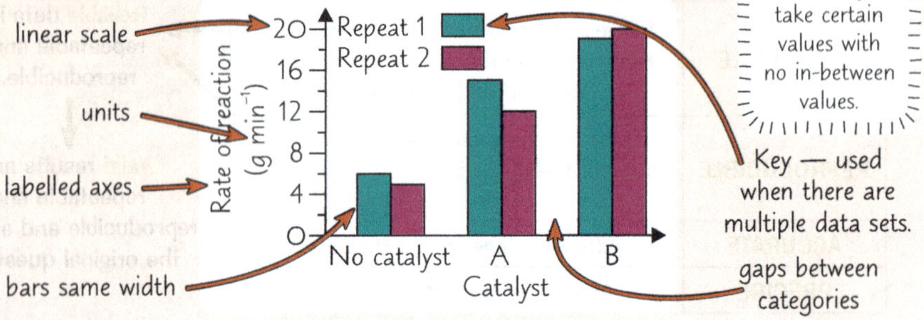

Key — used when there are multiple data sets.

gaps between categories

Plotting Graphs

Graphs can be used when both variables are continuous.

Continuous data — can take any numerical value within a range.

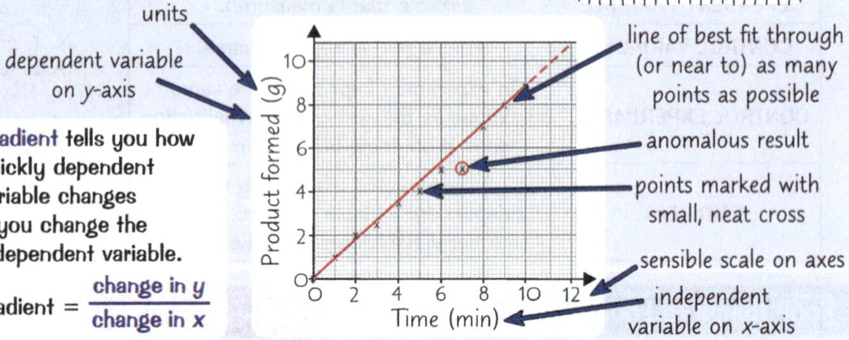

- units
- dependent variable on y-axis
- **Gradient** tells you how quickly dependent variable changes if you change the independent variable.

$$\text{gradient} = \frac{\text{change in } y}{\text{change in } x}$$

- line of best fit through (or near to) as many points as possible
- anomalous result
- points marked with small, neat cross
- sensible scale on axes
- independent variable on x-axis

Three Types of Correlation Between Variables

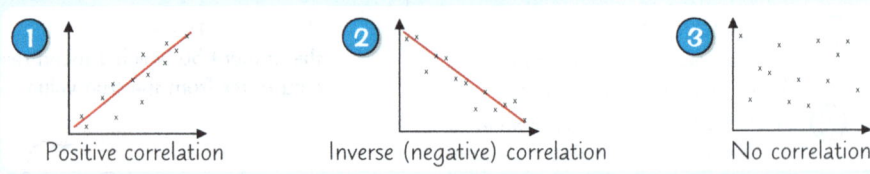

1. Positive correlation
2. Inverse (negative) correlation
3. No correlation

Possible reasons for a correlation:

Chance — correlation might be a fluke.

Third variable — another factor links the two variables.

Cause — if every other variable that could affect the result is controlled, you can conclude that changing one variable causes the change in the other.

Working Scientifically

Conclusions, Evaluations and Units

Conclusions

Draw conclusion by stating relationship between dependent and independent variables.

↓

Justify conclusion using specific data.

↓

Refer to original hypothesis and state whether data supports it.

You can only draw a conclusion from what your data shows — you can't go any further than that.

Evaluations

EVALUATION — a critical analysis of the whole investigation.

	Things to consider
Method	• Validity of method • Control of variables
Results	• Reliability, accuracy, precision and reproducibility of results • Number of measurements taken • Level of uncertainty in the results
Anomalous results	• Causes of any anomalous results

Repeating experiment with changes to improve the quality of results will give you more confidence in your conclusions.

You could make more predictions based on your conclusion, which you could test in future experiments.

S.I. Units

S.I. BASE UNITS — a set of standard units that all scientists use.

Quantity	S.I. Unit
mass	kilogram (kg)
length	metre (m)
time	second (s)
amount of a substance	mole (mol)

Scaling Units

SCALING PREFIX — a word or symbol that goes before a unit to indicate a multiplying factor.

Multiple of unit	Prefix
10^{12}	tera (T)
10^9	giga (G)
10^6	mega (M)
1000	kilo (k)
0.1	deci (d)
0.01	centi (c)
0.001	milli (m)
10^{-6}	micro (µ)
10^{-9}	nano (n)

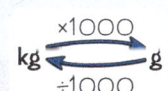

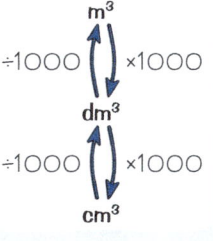

Working Scientifically

Topic 1 — Key Concepts in Chemistry

Chemical Equations

Chemical Formulas and Equations

CHEMICAL FORMULA — shows the proportion of atoms of each element in a compound.

E.g. CO_2 ← 2 oxygen atoms for every carbon atom

CHEMICAL EQUATION — shows the overall change in a reaction.

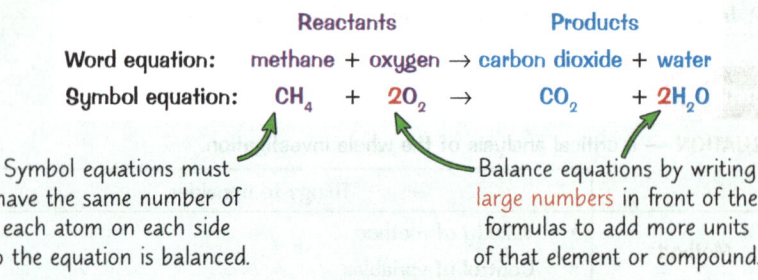

Reactants → Products

Word equation: methane + oxygen → carbon dioxide + water
Symbol equation: CH_4 + $2O_2$ → CO_2 + $2H_2O$

Symbol equations must have the same number of each atom on each side so the equation is balanced.

Balance equations by writing large numbers in front of the formulas to add more units of that element or compound.

State Symbols

(s)	solid
(l)	liquid
(g)	gas
(aq)	aqueous

'Aqueous' means dissolved in water.

Symbol of state.

Common Chemical Formulas

Name	Formula	Name	Formula
Water	H_2O	Ammonium	NH_4^+
Ammonia	NH_3	Hydroxide	OH^-
Carbon dioxide	CO_2	Nitrate	NO_3^-
Hydrogen	H_2	Carbonate	CO_3^{2-}
Chlorine	Cl_2	Sulfate	SO_4^{2-}
Oxygen	O_2		

Ionic Equations

IONIC EQUATIONS — show only the particles that react and the products they form.

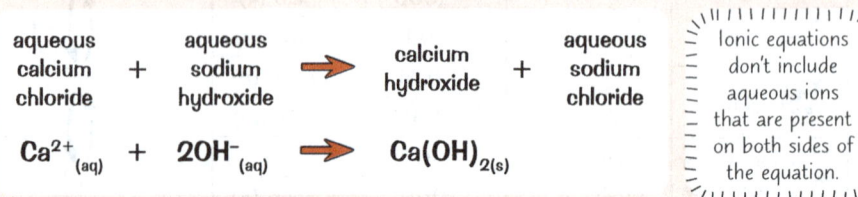

aqueous calcium chloride + aqueous sodium hydroxide → calcium hydroxide + aqueous sodium chloride

$Ca^{2+}_{(aq)}$ + $2OH^-_{(aq)}$ → $Ca(OH)_{2(s)}$

Ionic equations don't include aqueous ions that are present on both sides of the equation.

Topic 1 — Key Concepts in Chemistry

Hazards and History of the Atom

Hazard Symbols

HAZARD SYMBOLS — warn you about the dangers of a substance.

Understanding hazard symbols means you can use suitable safe-working procedures when working with the substances.

- Oxidising
- Corrosive
- Toxic
- Highly flammable
- Harmful
- Environmental hazard

When planning an experiment, do a risk assessment — identify the hazards and their risks, and suggest ways to reduce the risks.

The History of the Atom

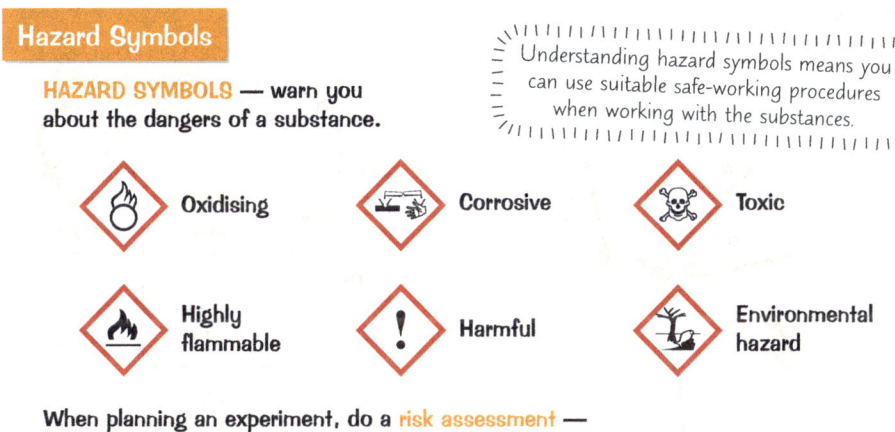

- **Start of 1800s** — John Dalton described atoms as solid spheres.
- **1897** — 'Plum pudding' model — ball of positive charge containing small negative electrons.
- **1909** — Nuclear model — a positive nucleus surrounded by a cloud of electrons (and mostly empty space). α-particles are fired at thin sheet... some are deflected backwards... most particles pass straight through.
- **1913** — Bohr model — electrons orbit nucleus in fixed shells.
- **Later experiments** — Nucleus contains protons that are positively charged and neutrons that are neutral.

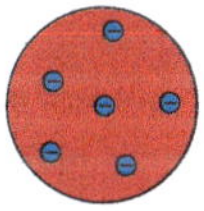

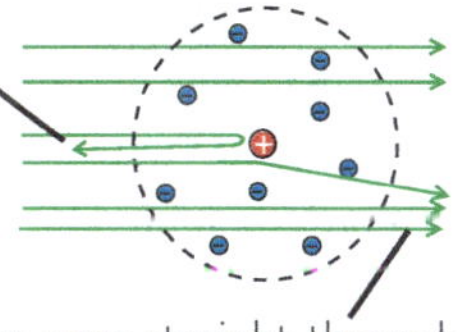

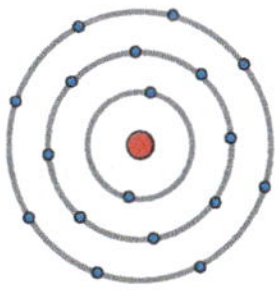

You don't need to worry about remembering specific dates.

Topic 1 — Key Concepts in Chemistry

Atoms, Elements and Isotopes

Atomic Structure

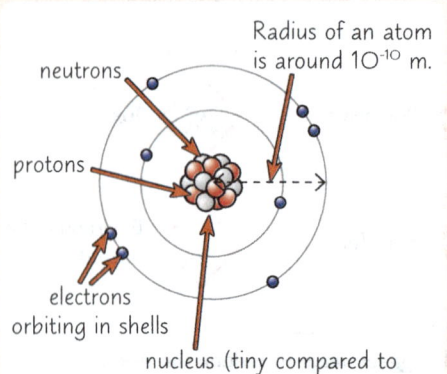

Radius of an atom is around 10^{-10} m.

- neutrons
- protons
- electrons orbiting in shells
- nucleus (tiny compared to overall size of atom)

Atoms have no overall charge because they have the same number of protons as electrons.

Particle	Relative mass	Relative charge
Proton	1	+1
Neutron	1	0
Electron	0.0005	−1

Most of the mass of an atom is in the nucleus.

Nuclear Symbols

NUCLEAR SYMBOL — used to describe atoms:

mass number = total number of protons and neutrons in an atom

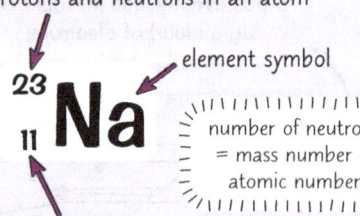

element symbol

number of neutrons = mass number − atomic number

atomic number = number of protons in an atom

Elements

ELEMENTS — substances made up of atoms with the same number of protons.

Different elements have different numbers of protons, so each element has a unique atomic number.

ISOTOPES of an element — atoms with the same number of protons but different numbers of neutrons.

Relative Atomic Mass

RELATIVE ATOMIC MASS (A_r) — the average mass of one atom of an element, compared to $\frac{1}{12}$ of the mass of one atom of carbon-12:

$$A_r = \frac{\text{sum of (isotope abundance} \times \text{isotope mass number)}}{\text{total abundance of all isotopes}}$$

A_r might not be a whole number because it's an average taking into account all the different isotopes.

Topic 1 — Key Concepts in Chemistry

The Periodic Table

Mendeleev's Table

Mendeleev made his Table of Elements by grouping elements using their properties.

If he ordered the elements by atomic mass, he could arrange them so his groups of elements with similar chemical properties formed columns.

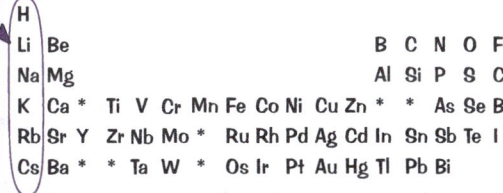

 Mendeleev swapped some elements round in places where ordering by atomic mass didn't fit the pattern.

 Some of the atomic masses he used were wrong due to the presence of isotopes.

 Mendeleev left gaps in the table to keep elements with similar properties together.

 He predicted the properties of missing elements using the other elements in the columns.

The Modern Periodic Table

Hydrogen is sometimes put in Group 1.

The elements are ordered by increasing atomic number.

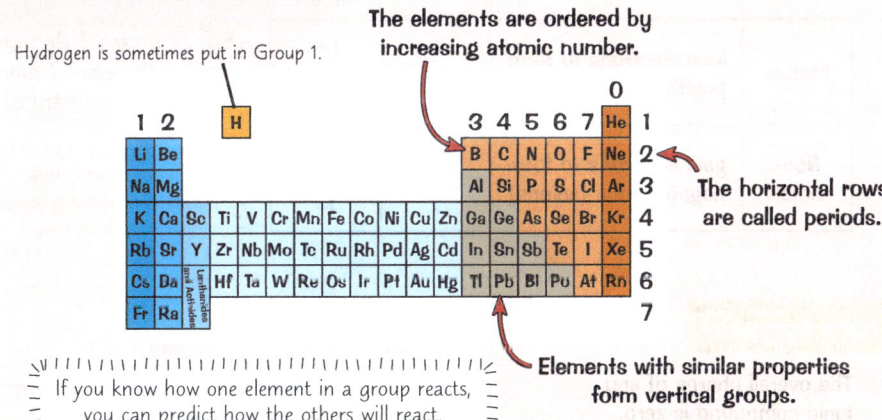

The horizontal rows are called periods.

Elements with similar properties form vertical groups.

If you know how one element in a group reacts, you can predict how the others will react.

Position in the periodic table tells you the electronic configuration:

Group number = the number of electrons in the outer shell.

Period number = the number of shells with electrons in.

Topic 1 — Key Concepts in Chemistry

Electronic Configurations and Ions

Electronic Configurations

Electrons occupy shells — sometimes called energy levels.
Electrons fill each shell up before occupying a new one, starting with the lowest energy.

Shell	Electrons allowed in shell
1	2
2	8
3	8

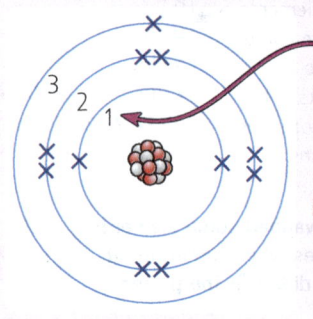

Lowest energy shells are closest to the nucleus.

Electronic configurations can also be represented using numbers — this one is **2.8.1**.

Forming Ions

IONS — charged particles made when electrons are transferred.

	Electron transfer	Group	Charge of ion
Metals	lose electrons to form positive ions (cations)	1	1+
		2	2+
Non-metals	gain electrons to form negative ions (anions)	6	2−
		7	1−

Charge on ion = number of electrons gained or lost.

E.g. 2+ means 2 electrons lost (so there are 2 more protons than electrons).

The ions formed by elements in these groups have full outer shells.

Ionic Formulas

The overall charge of any ionic compound is zero.

Calcium nitrate = Ca(NO$_3$)$_2$ (2+, 1−)

Overall charge is 0 as there are 2 nitrate ions for each calcium ion.

Name ends in...	Anion contains...
-ate	...oxygen and at least one other element.
-ide	...only one element.

Except for hydroxide ions, OH$^-$.

Topic 1 — Key Concepts in Chemistry

Ionic Substances and Bonding Models

Ionic Bonding

IONIC BONDING — the electrostatic attraction between oppositely charged ions. Ionic bonds form when electrons are transferred from metal atoms to non-metal atoms.

Sodium Chloride

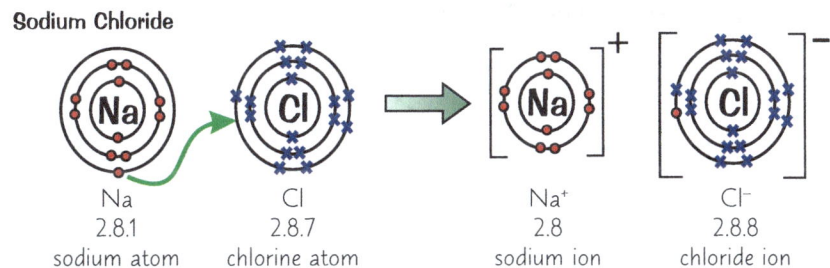

Na	Cl	Na⁺	Cl⁻
2.8.1	2.8.7	2.8	2.8.8
sodium atom	chlorine atom	sodium ion	chloride ion

Giant Ionic Lattice

Strong electrostatic forces of attraction between oppositely charged ions act in all directions.

Closely-packed regular arrangement of ions.

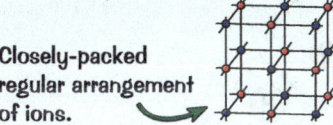

Three Properties of Ionic Compounds

①  High melting and boiling points — lots of energy needed to overcome the strong attraction between the ions.

② Soluble in water.

③ Conduct electricity only when molten or dissolved — ions free to move and carry electric charge.

Models

Ball and stick diagrams.

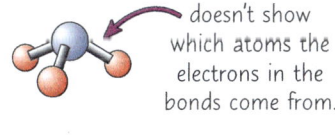 doesn't show which atoms the electrons in the bonds come from.

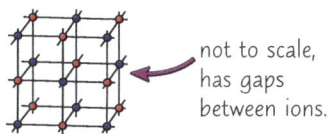 not to scale, has gaps between ions.

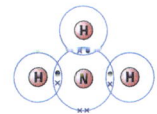 Dot and cross diagrams — don't show relative sizes of atoms or their arrangement in space.

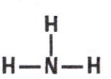 Displayed formula (2D) — doesn't show 3D structure or sizes of atoms.

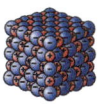 3D model — only shows outer layer.

Topic 1 — Key Concepts in Chemistry

Molecular Substances

Simple Molecular Substances

COVALENT BOND — a shared pair of electrons between two non-metal atoms.

Simple molecular substances are made up of molecules containing a few covalently-bonded atoms.

Elements

Hydrogen (H_2)

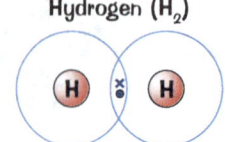

Oxygen (O_2)

size of a simple molecule is around 10^{-10} m

Compounds

Hydrogen chloride (HCl)

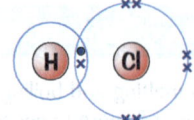

Carbon dioxide (CO_2)

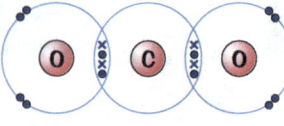

Covalent bonds between atoms are strong. Forces between molecules are weak.

Methane (CH_4)

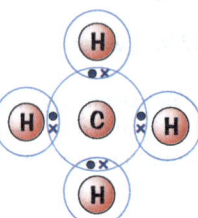

Water (H_2O)

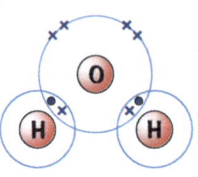

Three Properties of Simple Molecular Substances

1 Low melting and boiling points — mostly gases or liquids at room temperature.

2  Don't conduct electricity — there are no charged particles to carry charge.

3 Some are soluble in water, and some aren't.

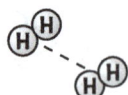

As molecules get smaller, less energy is needed to break the weaker forces between them.

These properties are also typical of non-metal elements.

Topic 1 — Key Concepts in Chemistry

More Covalent Substances

Giant Covalent Structures

GIANT COVALENT STRUCTURES — solids containing atoms which are all bonded to each other by strong covalent bonds.

 High melting and boiling points — lots of energy needed to overcome strong covalent bonds.

 Don't conduct electricity (with a couple of exceptions) — no charged particles to carry charge.

 Not soluble in water.

Examples include diamond and graphite.

Polymers

POLYMERS — very long chains of covalently bonded carbon atoms.

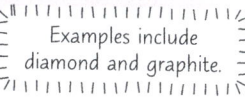

poly(ethene)

strong covalent bonds

'n' is a large number.

Carbon Allotropes

	Diamond 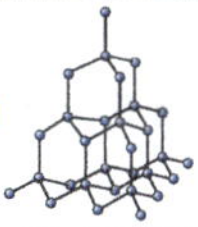	Graphite 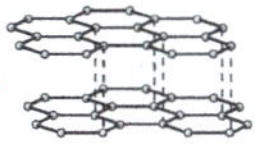	Graphene 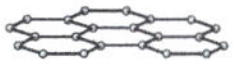
Bonding	C atoms form four covalent bonds	C atoms form three covalent bonds. No covalent bonds between layers	C atoms form three covalent bonds
Properties	Very hard	Soft, slippery	Strong, light
Conductivity	Doesn't conduct electricity	Conducts electricity and thermal energy	Conducts electricity
Uses	Cutting tools	Electrodes, lubricant	

Each carbon atom in graphite and graphene has one delocalised electron.

FULLERENES — have hollow shapes, giving them large surface areas.

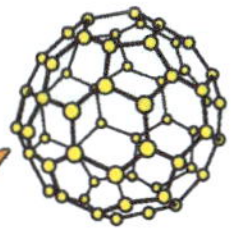

rings of 6 carbon atoms (sometimes 5 or 7)

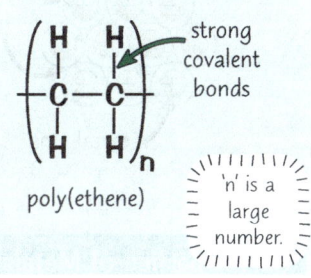

Buckminsterfullerene (C_{60}) is spherical.

Nanotubes are cylindrical fullerenes. They have delocalised electrons so they can conduct electricity.

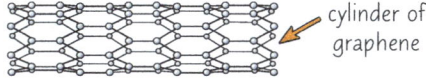

cylinder of graphene

Topic 1 — Key Concepts in Chemistry

Metallic Bonding, Metals & Non-Metals

Metallic Bonding

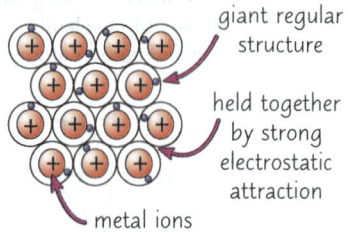
giant regular structure
held together by strong electrostatic attraction
metal ions

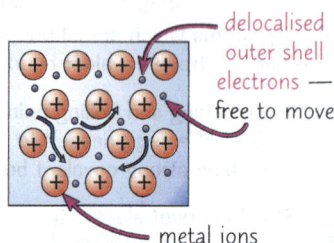
delocalised outer shell electrons — free to move
metal ions

Six Properties of Metals

 **1** High melting and boiling points as lots of energy needed to overcome strong metallic bonds. Generally solids at room temperature.

 2 High density — ions are packed close together.

 **3** Not soluble in water.

 **4** Shiny appearance.

 **5** Good electrical conductors — delocalised electrons carry charge.

 **6** Soft and malleable — layers in metals slide over each other.

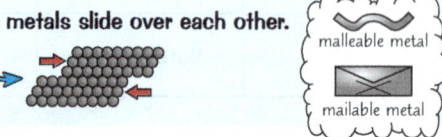
malleable metal
mailable metal

Chemical Properties of Metals and Non-Metals

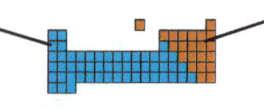

METALS — outer shell under half-filled, lose electrons to get a full outer shell.

NON-METALS — outer shell over half-filled, gain electrons to get a full outer shell.

Topic 1 — Key Concepts in Chemistry

Mass, Moles and Limiting Reactants

Relative Formula Mass

RELATIVE FORMULA MASS (M_r) — sum of all the relative atomic masses (A_r) of the atoms in the molecular formula.

The Mole

One mole = 6.02×10^{23} particles of a substance.
This is the Avogadro constant.

Guacamole recipe: take 6.02×10^{23} avocados...

The particles could be e.g. atoms, molecules or ions.

Mass in grams of one mole of atoms of an element = the A_r of the element.

Mass in grams of one mole of molecules of a compound = the M_r of the compound.

Number of moles (mol) = $\dfrac{\text{mass in g}}{M_r \text{ or } A_r}$

To find the number of particles in a given mass, first find the number of moles.

Number of particles = moles $\times 6.02 \times 10^{23}$

Balancing Equations Using Masses

If you know the masses of reactants and products:

Divide mass by M_r to find the number of moles of each substance.
↓
Divide each number of moles by the smallest number of moles.
↓
If results aren't all whole numbers, multiply them by the same number so that they are whole.
↓
Put these numbers in front of the chemical formulas.

Limiting Reactants

LIMITING REACTANT — a reactant that gets completely used up in a reaction, so limits the amount of product formed.

All the other reactants are in excess.

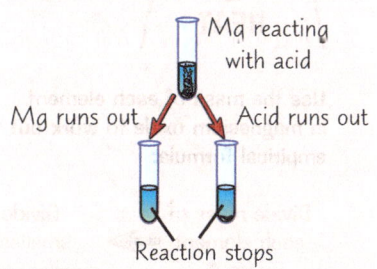

Mg reacting with acid
Mg runs out — Acid runs out
Reaction stops

Topic 1 — Key Concepts in Chemistry

Concentration and Empirical Formulas

Concentration

CONCENTRATION — amount of substance dissolved in a certain volume of solution.

Increase the...	Concentration...
...amount of solute	...increases
...volume of solution	...decreases

$$\text{Concentration} = \frac{\text{mass of solute}}{\text{volume of solution}}$$

Units = $g\ dm^{-3}$

Empirical Formula

EMPIRICAL FORMULA — the smallest whole number ratio of atoms in a compound.

molecular formula ⟷ empirical formula
$C_6H_{12}O_6$ CH_2O

To find molecular formula from empirical formula:

Find M_r of empirical formula.
↓
Divide M_r of compound by M_r of empirical formula.
↓
Multiply atoms in empirical formula by result.

Empirical Formula Experiment

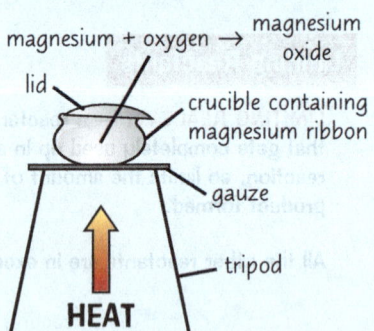

magnesium + oxygen → magnesium oxide

lid, crucible containing magnesium ribbon, gauze, tripod, HEAT

You need to weigh:

① Empty crucible and its lid.

② Crucible, lid and contents before heating.

③ Crucible, lid and contents after heating.

Mass of magnesium = ② − ①

Mass of oxygen = ③ − ②

This method works for any compound if you know how much of each element is present.

Use the mass of each element in magnesium oxide to work out empirical formula:

Divide mass of each element by its A_r. → Divide each result by smallest number to get smallest whole number ratio. → This gives the number of atoms of each element in empirical formula.

Topic 1 — Key Concepts in Chemistry

Equations and Conservation of Mass

Calculating Masses Using Balanced Equations

To work out the mass of product formed from a given mass of a reactant:

Write a balanced equation for the reaction.
⬇
Divide the mass of the reactant by its M_r to find the number of moles.
⬇
Use the balanced equation to find the number of moles of the product.
⬇
Multiply this number of moles by the M_r of the product to work out its mass.

This is assuming that all the reactant gets used up in the reaction.

Cong writes his balanced equations unconventionally.

You can also find the mass of a reactant from the mass of a product using this method.

Conservation of Mass

No atoms are created or destroyed in a chemical reaction, so the total masses of reactants and products are also the same — MASS IS CONSERVED.

If you weigh a sealed reaction vessel, you shouldn't see a change in mass:

No reactants or products can escape.

Mass doesn't change.

E.g. a precipitation reaction.

If you weigh an unsealed reaction vessel, sometimes you'll see a change in mass:

DECREASE in mass
— a gas is made during the reaction and escapes the vessel, so its mass is no longer accounted for.

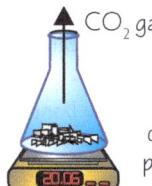

CO_2 gas escapes

E.g. the thermal decomposition of calcium carbonate produces CO_2 gas.

INCREASE in mass
— a gas from the air is a reactant, so its mass is added to the mass in the vessel (none of the products are gaseous).

O_2 gas enters

E.g. the reaction of magnesium with O_2 gas only produces a solid.

Topic 1 — Key Concepts in Chemistry

Topic 2 — States of Matter and Mixtures

States of Matter

Particle Model

	Solid	Liquid	Gas
Particle Diagram			
Particle Arrangement	Regular	Random	Random
Particle Movement	Fixed position, can vibrate	Move around each other	Move quickly in all directions
Relative Energy of Particles	Low	Medium	High

Changes of State

Changes between states of matter are physical changes.

The change from liquid to gas at the surface of a liquid is called evaporation.

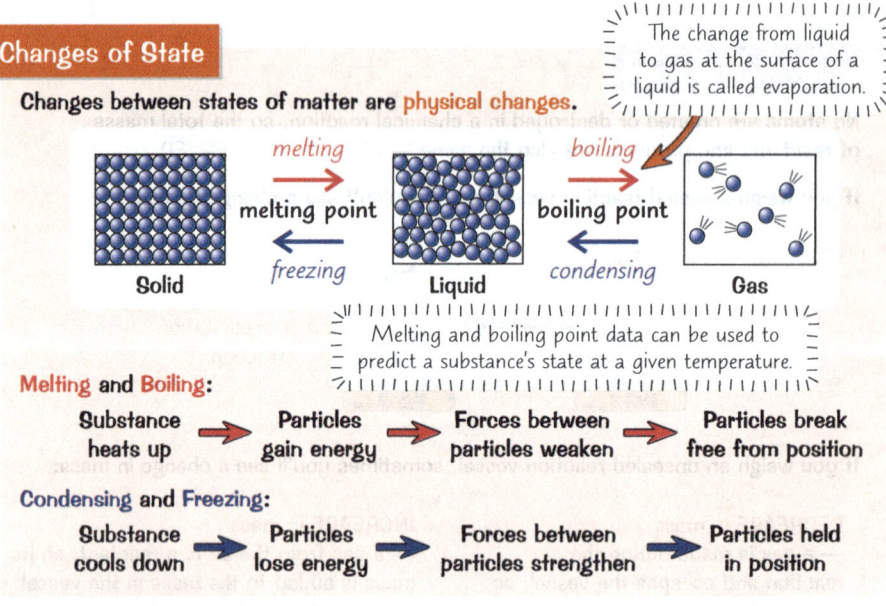

Melting and boiling point data can be used to predict a substance's state at a given temperature.

Melting and **Boiling**:

Substance heats up → Particles gain energy → Forces between particles weaken → Particles break free from position

Condensing and **Freezing**:

Substance cools down → Particles lose energy → Forces between particles strengthen → Particles held in position

Chemical Changes

Chemical changes happen in chemical reactions.

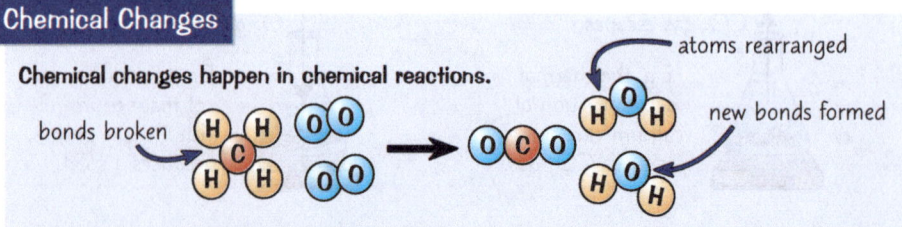

Purity

Definitions of Purity

	Everyday Definition	Chemical Definition
PURE SUBSTANCE	Clean or natural.	A substance containing only one element or compound.

Pure Substances

A chemically pure substance will:

 Have a sharp melting point.

 Have a sharp boiling point.

You can measure the melting point of a substance using melting point apparatus, or with a water bath and thermometer.

thermometer — sample
block heats sample

Mixtures

MIXTURES — substances made up of different elements or compounds that aren't chemically bonded to each other.

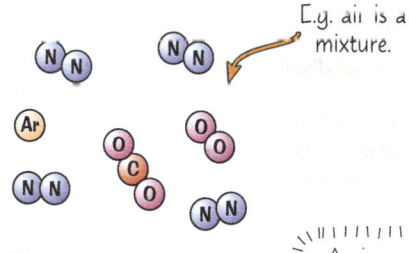

E.g. air is a mixture.

Mixtures melt gradually over a range of temperatures.

An impure substance is a mixture, so it will melt over a range of temperatures.

Topic 2 — States of Matter and Mixtures

Separation Techniques

Filtration

FILTRATION — separates insoluble solids from liquids and solutions.

It can be used to separate out a solid product, or purify a liquid by removing insoluble impurities.

filter paper
Solid left in the filter paper.

Evaporation

EVAPORATION — separates soluble salts from solution.

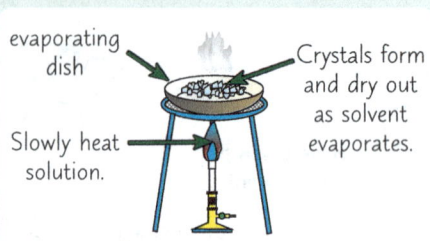
evaporating dish
Crystals form and dry out as solvent evaporates.
Slowly heat solution.

Crystallisation

CRYSTALLISATION — also separates soluble salts from solution.

Heat solution, but cool it when crystals start to form.
⬇
Large crystals form as solution cools.
⬇
Filter out crystals and leave to dry.

Two Types of Distillation

① **Simple** distillation

The part with the lowest boiling point evaporates first.

Simple distillation can't separate liquids with similar boiling points, but fractional distillation can.

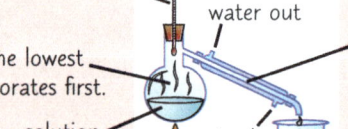
thermometer
water out
Vapour is cooled and condenses.
solution
water in
heat
pure liquid

② **Fractional** distillation

Liquids reach the top of the column when the temperature at the top matches their boiling point.

fractionating column filled with glass rods

thermometer
condenser
fractions collected separately
mixture of liquids
heat

Topic 2 — States of Matter and Mixtures

Chromatography

Paper Chromatography

CHROMATOGRAPHY — a method used to separate a mixture of soluble substances.

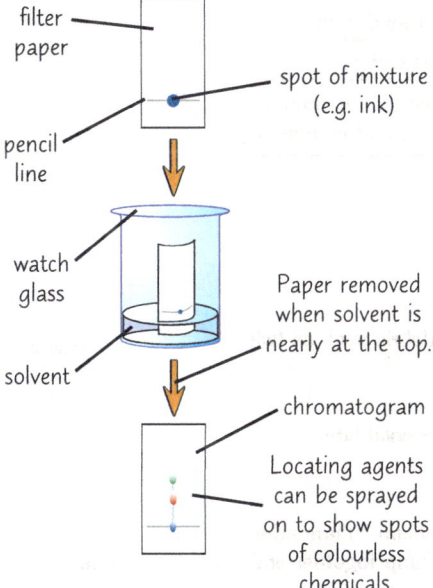

Two Phases of Chromatography

1 STATIONARY PHASE — where the molecules can't move.
e.g. chromatography paper

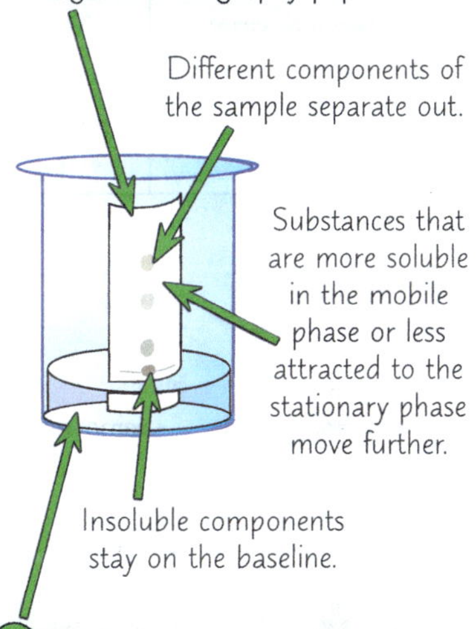

Different components of the sample separate out.

Substances that are more soluble in the mobile phase or less attracted to the stationary phase move further.

Insoluble components stay on the baseline.

2 MOBILE PHASE — where the molecules can move (the solvent).
e.g. water or ethanol

R_f Values

R_f VALUE — the ratio between the distance travelled by the solute and the distance travelled by the solvent.

$$R_f = \frac{\text{distance travelled by solute (B)}}{\text{distance travelled by solvent (A)}}$$

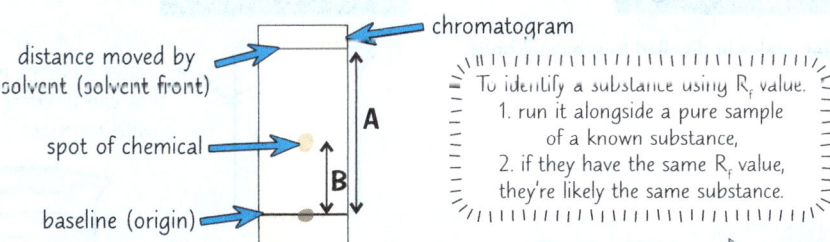

To identify a substance using R_f value.
1. run it alongside a pure sample of a known substance,
2. if they have the same R_f value, they're likely the same substance.

Lou was excited to calculate his Ref value.

Chromatography can be used for purity tests. Pure substances won't separate in chromatography — they move as one spot.

Topic 2 — States of Matter and Mixtures

Water Treatment

Sources of Water

POTABLE WATER — water that is safe to drink.

Type of Water	Source
Ground water	Underground rocks
Salt water	Sea water
Waste water	Water contaminated by a human process, e.g. as a by-product in industry

Potable water is not chemically pure. It can contain low levels of dissolved salts and microbes.

Treating Water

This is how waste water and ground water are made potable.

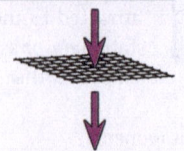

Mesh
— removes any large debris such as twigs.

Sand and gravel filtration
— removes any smaller solid bits.

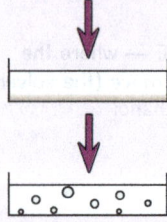

Sedimentation
— iron sulfate or aluminium sulfate added to water, making fine particles clump together and settle at bottom.

Chlorination
— chlorine gas bubbled through to kill harmful bacteria and other microbes.

Distilling Sea Water

Sea water is distilled in areas without much fresh water to make it potable.

DISTILLATION — boiling the water to separate it from dissolved salts.

This uses lots of energy.

Water for Analysis

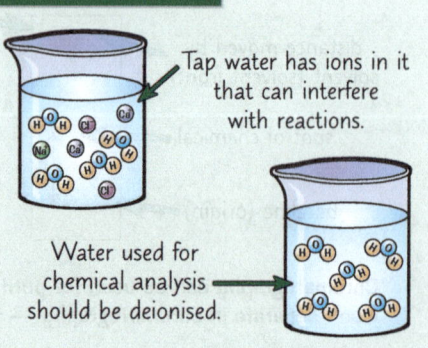

Tap water has ions in it that can interfere with reactions.

Water used for chemical analysis should be deionised.

Topic 2 — States of Matter and Mixtures

Topic 3 — Chemical Changes

Acids and Bases

The pH Scale

Alkalis are soluble bases.

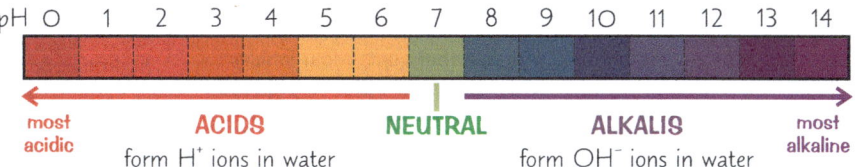

pH 0 1 2 3 4 5 6 7 8 9 10 11 12 13 14

← most acidic ... **ACIDS** form H⁺ ions in water ... **NEUTRAL** ... **ALKALIS** form OH⁻ ions in water ... most alkaline →

higher H⁺ concentration = lower pH   higher OH⁻ concentration = higher pH

Indicators

	Colour when solution is...		
	acidic	neutral	alkaline
litmus	red	purple	blue
methyl orange	red	yellow	yellow
phenol-phthalein	colourless	colourless	pink

Neutralisation Reactions

Any substance that reacts with acid this way is a base.

acid + base ⟶ salt + water

The products of neutralisation reactions are neutral.

$H^+_{(aq)} + OH^-_{(aq)} \rightarrow H_2O_{(l)}$

Acid Used	Salt Produced
HCl	chloride
H_2SO_4	sulfate
HNO_3	nitrate

Reactions of Acids

acid + metal oxide ⟶ salt + water
acid + metal hydroxide ⟶ salt + water
acid + metal carbonate ⟶ salt + water + carbon dioxide
acid + metal ⟶ salt + hydrogen

To test for hydrogen: POP! lighted splint, H_2 gas in open test tube

To test for carbon dioxide: CO_2 gas → limewater → limewater turns cloudy

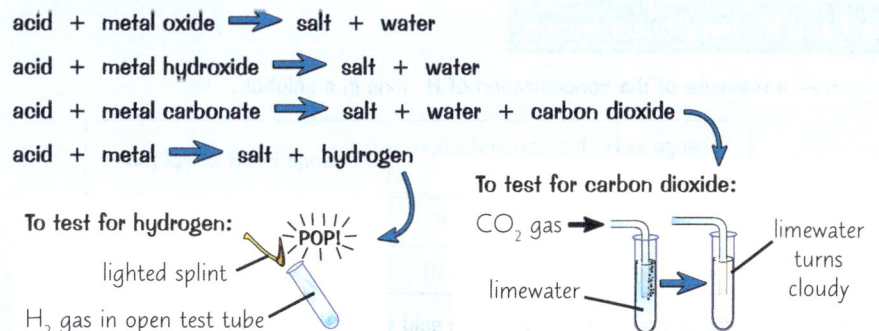

Strong and Weak Acids

Acid Strength

	Definition	Examples
STRONG ACID	An acid that completely ionises (dissociates) in water to produce hydrogen ions. E.g. HCl → H$^+$ + Cl$^-$	hydrochloric acid sulfuric acid nitric acid
WEAK ACID	An acid that partially ionises (dissociates) in water to produce hydrogen ions. E.g. CH$_3$COOH ⇌ H$^+$ + CH$_3$COO$^-$	ethanoic acid citric acid carbonic acid

Strength vs Concentration

	A measure of...
ACID **STRENGTH**	...the proportion of acid molecules that ionise in water.
ACID **CONCENTRATION**	...the number of acid molecules in a certain volume of water.

Dilute acids have a low concentration.
Concentrated acids have a high concentration.

The pH will decrease with increasing acid concentration regardless of whether it's a strong or weak acid.

pH and H$^+$ Ion Concentration

pH — a measure of the concentration of H$^+$ ions in a solution.

Change in H$^+$ ion concentration of solution	Change in pH of solution
↑ increases by a factor of 10	↓ decreases by 1
↓ decreases by a factor of 10	↑ increases by 1

For a given concentration of acid, as the acid strength increases, pH decreases.

Topic 3 — Chemical Changes

Insoluble and Soluble Salts

Solubility

You can use these rules to predict whether a product will be aqueous or a precipitate.

Substance	Soluble?	
common salts of sodium, potassium and ammonium	yes	
nitrates	yes	
common chlorides	yes	(except silver chloride and lead chloride)
common sulfates	yes	(except lead, barium and calcium sulfate)
common carbonates and hydroxides	no	(except for sodium, potassium and ammonium ones)

Making Insoluble Salts

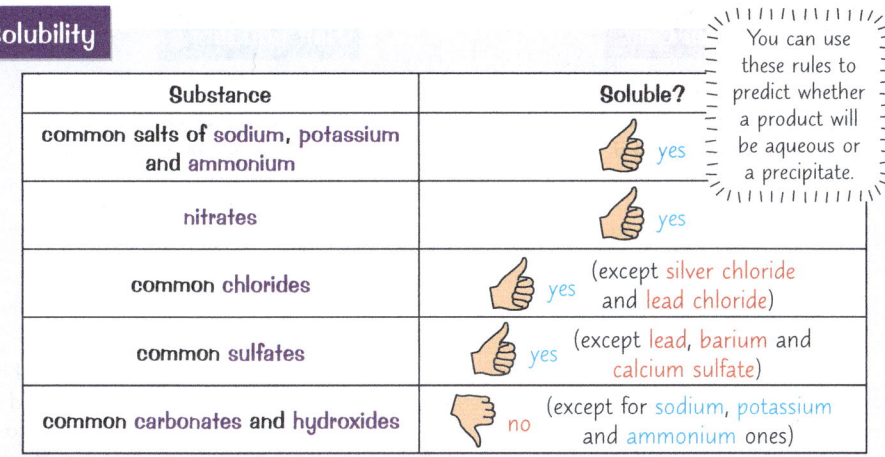

soluble salts in solution — precipitate — filter paper — filter funnel — insolent salt — dry precipitate

Making Soluble Salts

acid + insoluble base:

Excess insoluble base added to acid, so all the acid reacts.

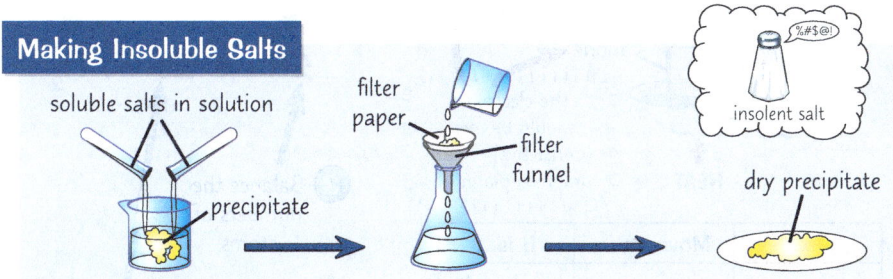

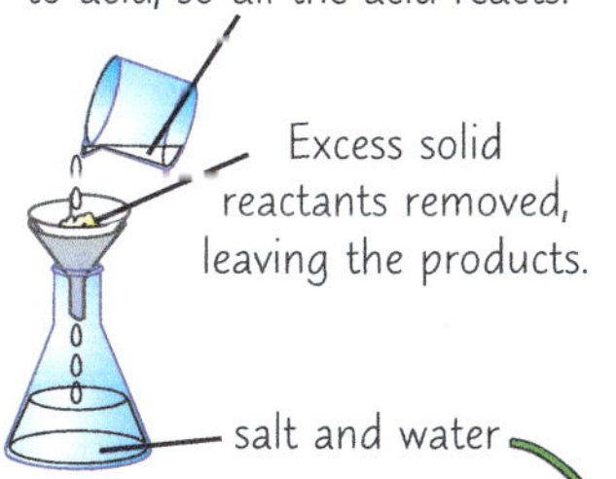

Excess solid reactants removed, leaving the products. — salt and water

acid + soluble base:

The acid is measured using a pipette.

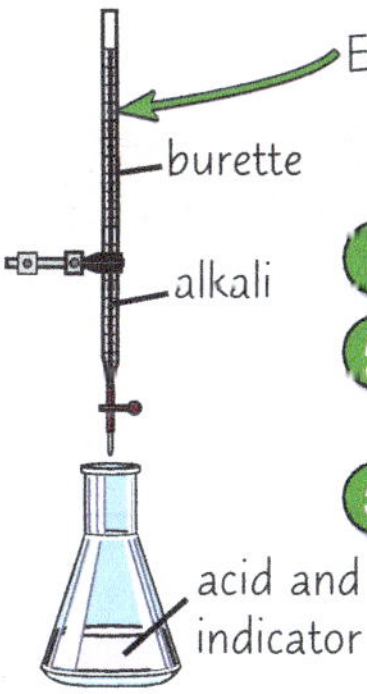

Excess reactants can't be removed, so titration is used to find the exact amounts to react.

— burette
— alkali
— acid and indicator

1. Slowly add alkali to acid.
2. Stop when indicator changes colour (the end point).
3. Repeat with the same volumes of acid and alkali but no indicator to get a solution of salt and water.

Heat the salt and water solution gently to crystallise the salt, then filter off the crystals and leave them to dry.

Topic 3 — Chemical Changes

Electrolysis

Electrochemical Cells

ELECTROLYSIS — passing an electric current through an electrolyte, causing it to decompose.

Electrolyte — a molten or dissolved ionic compound.

Electrolyte = dissolved ionic compound:

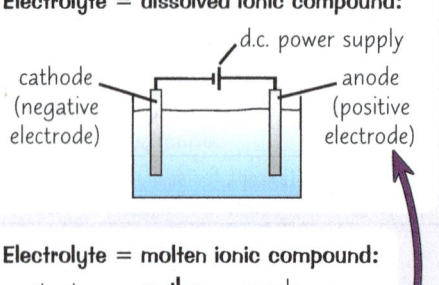

Electrolyte = molten ionic compound:

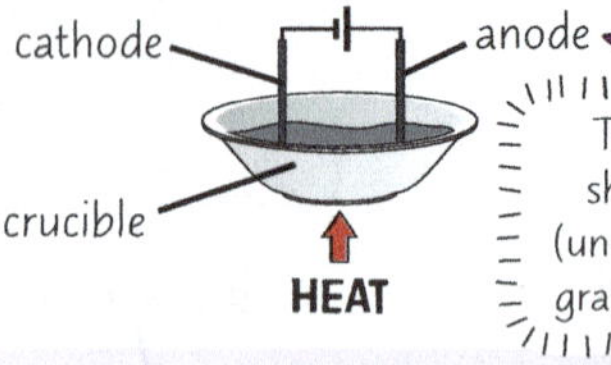

The electrodes should be inert (unreactive) — e.g. graphite, platinum.

Ion	Moves to...	It is...
cation (+ve)	cathode (−ve)	reduced (gains e−)
anion (−ve)	anode (+ve)	oxidised (loses e−)

Half Equations

HALF EQUATIONS — show how electrons are transferred during reactions.

To write a half equation:

1. Write the thing being oxidised or reduced.
2. Write the thing it is oxidised or reduced to.

$$2H^+ + 2e^- \rightarrow H_2$$

3. Balance the numbers of atoms.
4. Add electrons to balance the charges.

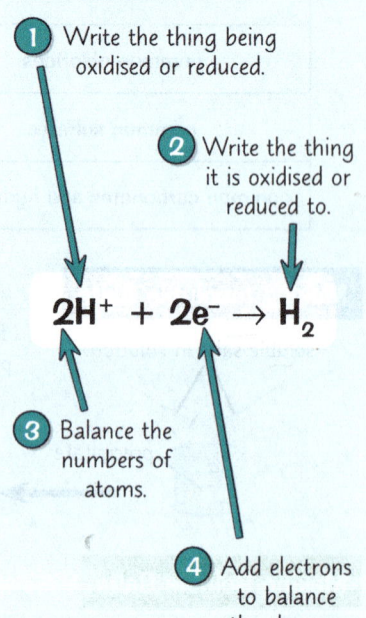

Electrolysis of Molten Ionic Compounds

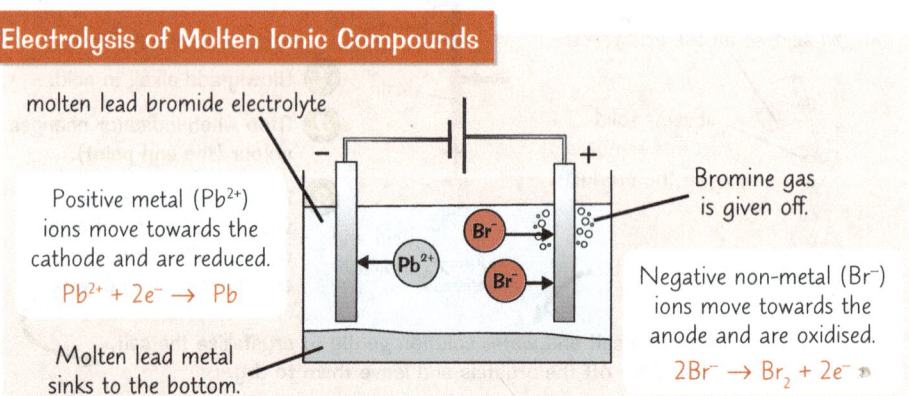

molten lead bromide electrolyte

Positive metal (Pb^{2+}) ions move towards the cathode and are reduced.
$Pb^{2+} + 2e^- \rightarrow Pb$

Molten lead metal sinks to the bottom.

Bromine gas is given off.

Negative non-metal (Br^-) ions move towards the anode and are oxidised.
$2Br^- \rightarrow Br_2 + 2e^-$

Topic 3 — Chemical Changes

More on Electrolysis

Electrolysis of Aqueous Ionic Compounds

Metal produced at cathode if it is less reactive than H_2.

If metal is more reactive than H_2, H_2 is produced at cathode.

Halogen produced at anode if halide ions are present.

If no halide ions are present, O_2 and H_2O are produced at anode.

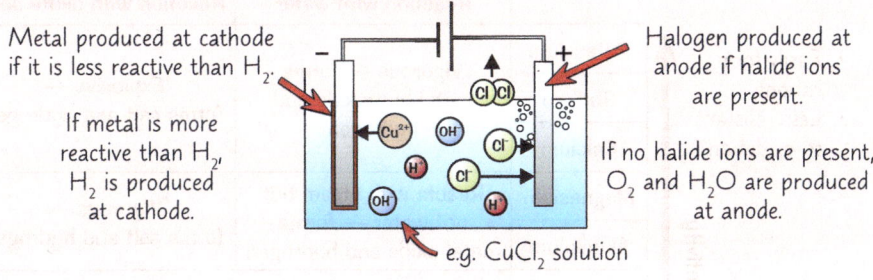

e.g. $CuCl_2$ solution

Aqueous Electrolyte	Product at Cathode	Product at Anode
Copper chloride $CuCl_2$	Copper $Cu^{2+} + 2e^- \rightarrow Cu$	Chlorine $2Cl^- \rightarrow Cl_2 + 2e^-$
Sodium chloride $NaCl$	Hydrogen $2H^+ + 2e^- \rightarrow H_2$	Chlorine $2Cl^- \rightarrow Cl_2 + 2e^-$
Sodium sulfate Na_2SO_4	Hydrogen $2H^+ + 2e^- \rightarrow H_2$	Oxygen and water $4OH^- \rightarrow O_2 + 2H_2O + 4e^-$
Water acidified with sulfuric acid H_2O/H_2SO_4	Hydrogen $2H^+ + 2e^- \rightarrow H_2$	Oxygen and water $4OH^- \rightarrow O_2 + 2H_2O + 4e^-$

Purifying Copper

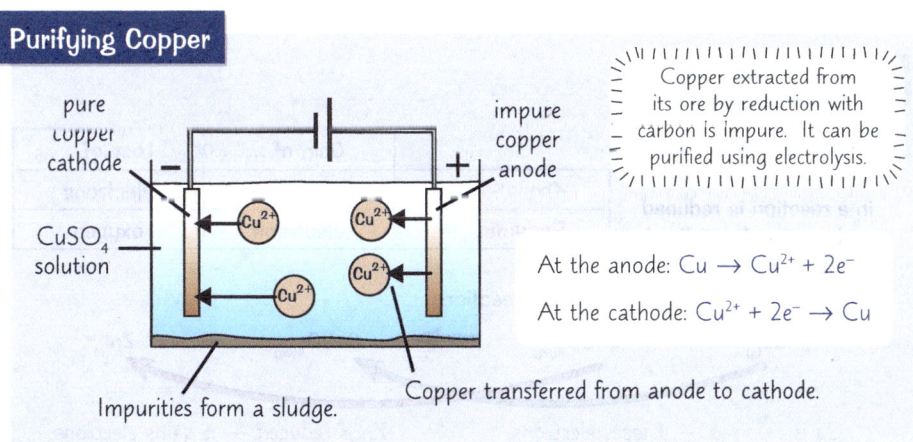

Copper extracted from its ore by reduction with carbon is impure. It can be purified using electrolysis.

At the anode: $Cu \rightarrow Cu^{2+} + 2e^-$

At the cathode: $Cu^{2+} + 2e^- \rightarrow Cu$

Copper transferred from anode to cathode.

Impurities form a sludge.

Topic 3 — Chemical Changes

Reactivity of Metals

The Reactivity Series

- Easily form cations.
- Less resistant to oxidation.

↑ increasing reactivity

- Do not easily form cations.
- More resistant to oxidation.

	Reaction with water	Reaction with dilute acid
Potassium	Vigorous — forms metal hydroxide and hydrogen	Explosive — forms salt and hydrogen
Sodium		
Calcium		
Magnesium	Reacts with steam but not water — forms metal oxide and hydrogen	Vigorous — forms salt and hydrogen
Aluminium		
CARBON		
Zinc	Reacts with steam but not water — forms metal oxide and hydrogen	Some bubbling — forms salt and hydrogen
Iron		
HYDROGEN		
Copper	No reaction	No reaction
Silver		
Gold		

DISPLACEMENT REACTION — when a more reactive element takes the place of a less reactive metal in a compound.

You can use the reactions with acid and water, plus displacement reactions, to find a metal's position in the reactivity series.

Redox Reactions

REDOX REACTION — where one substance in a reaction is reduced and another is oxidised.

	Gain of...	or	Loss of...
Oxidation =	oxygen		electrons
Reduction =	electrons		oxygen

Displacement reactions are redox reactions.

$Ca_{(s)} + ZnSO_{4(aq)} \rightarrow CaSO_{4(aq)} + Zn_{(s)}$

Ca is oxidised — it loses electrons.   Zn is reduced — it gains electrons.

Extracting Metals

Extraction Methods

Most metals are extracted from ores taken from the Earth's crust.

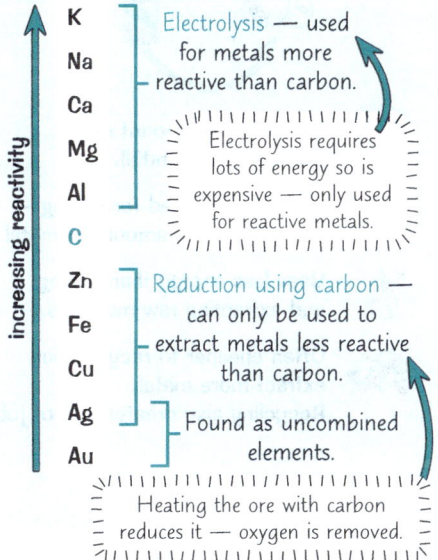

- K
- Na
- Ca — Electrolysis — used for metals more reactive than carbon.
- Mg
- Al
- C

Electrolysis requires lots of energy so is expensive — only used for reactive metals.

- Zn
- Fe — Reduction using carbon — can only be used to extract metals less reactive than carbon.
- Cu
- Ag — Found as uncombined elements.
- Au

Heating the ore with carbon reduces it — oxygen is removed.

(increasing reactivity)

Extraction by Electrolysis

E.g. extraction of aluminium:

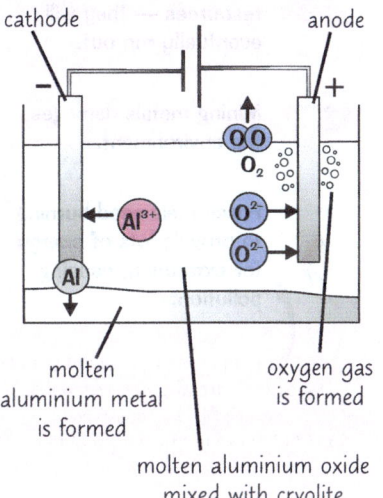

cathode — anode
O_2
Al^{3+}
O^{2-}
O^{2-}
Al

molten aluminium metal is formed

oxygen gas is formed

molten aluminium oxide mixed with cryolite (to lower the melting point)

Biological Methods of Extraction

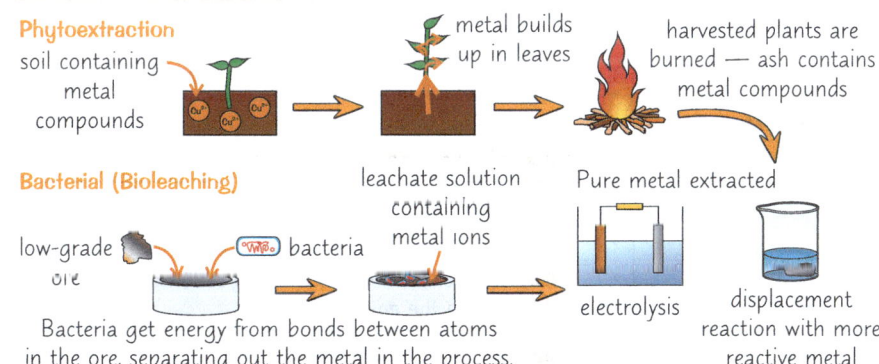

Phytoextraction
soil containing metal compounds → metal builds up in leaves → harvested plants are burned — ash contains metal compounds

Bacterial (Bioleaching)
low-grade ore + bacteria → leachate solution containing metal ions → Pure metal extracted (electrolysis / displacement reaction with more reactive metal)

Bacteria get energy from bonds between atoms in the ore, separating out the metal in the process.

Compared to traditional methods:
- ✓ Can be used to extract metals from low-grade ores or from waste.
- ✓ Less damaging to environment.
- ✗ Slow.

Topic 4 — Extracting Metals and Equilibria

Recycling and Life Cycle Assessments

Issues With Extracting Metals

Metals are non-renewable resources — they will eventually run out.

Mining metals damages the environment.

Fossil fuels need burning to provide lots of energy for extraction, causing pollution.

Fossil fuels are also non-renewable, so need to be conserved.

Benefits of Recycling Metals

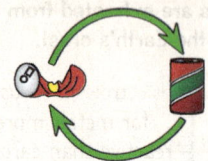

Reduces the amount of waste sent to landfill.

Reduces the need for mining — preserves finite amount of metal.

Uses less energy than mining and extracting raw materials.

Often cheaper to recycle than extract more metal.
Recycling also creates lots of jobs.

Life Cycle Assessments

LIFE CYCLE ASSESSMENT (LCA) — an assessment of the environmental impact of a product over each stage of its life.

Life Cycle Assessment Stage	Considerations
Raw Materials	• Metals need mining and extraction from ores. • Raw materials for chemical manufacture often come from crude oil (non-renewable resource).
Manufacturing	• Uses a lot of energy and can cause pollution. • Waste products need recycling or disposing of. • Polluted water from manufacturing processes shouldn't be put back into the environment.
Using the Product	• Could damage the environment, e.g. by releasing toxic fumes or greenhouse gases, or by contaminating streams and rivers.
Product Disposal	• Disposal in landfill takes up space and can cause pollution. • Incineration causes air pollution.

Topic 4 — Extracting Metals and Equilibria

Reversible Reactions

Equilibrium

DYNAMIC EQUILIBRIUM — the forward and backward reactions are both happening at the **same rate**.

Reversible reaction — where the products can react to form the reactants again.

Equilibrium can only be reached when a reversible reaction takes place in a closed system (where nothing can enter or leave).

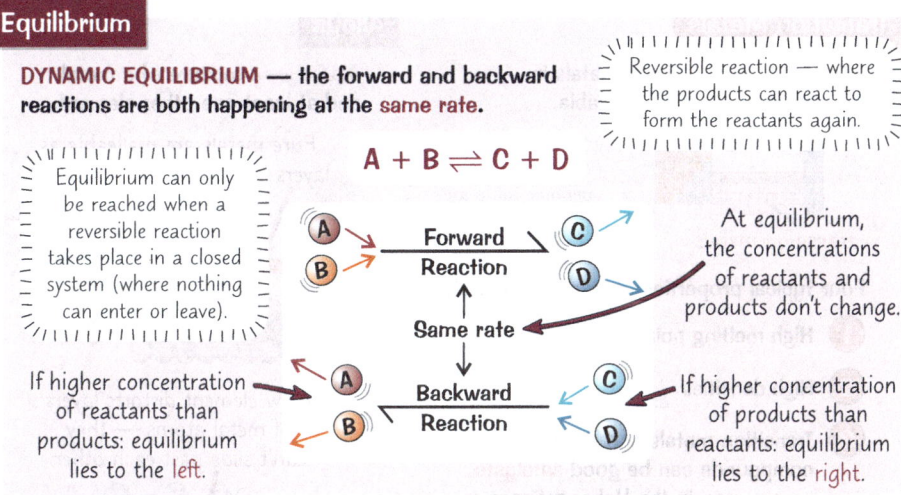

$$A + B \rightleftharpoons C + D$$

At equilibrium, the concentrations of reactants and products don't change.

If higher concentration of reactants than products: equilibrium lies to the **left**.

If higher concentration of products than reactants: equilibrium lies to the **right**.

Haber Process

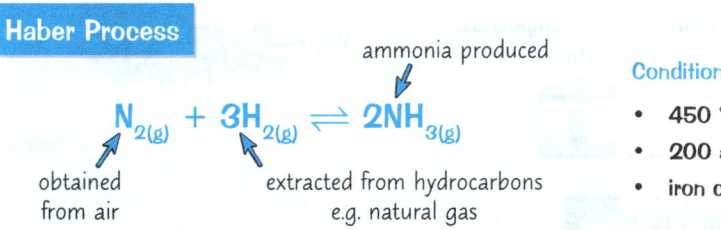

ammonia produced

$$N_{2(g)} + 3H_{2(g)} \rightleftharpoons 2NH_{3(g)}$$

obtained from air

extracted from hydrocarbons e.g. natural gas

Conditions:
- 450 °C
- 200 atmospheres
- iron catalyst

Le Chatelier's Principle

If the conditions of a reversible reaction at equilibrium are changed, the system tries to counteract that change.

If the reaction is endothermic in one direction, it will be exothermic in the other.

		The equilibrium shifts to favour the...
Temperature	increases	...endothermic direction to take in heat energy.
	decreases	...exothermic direction to release heat energy.
Pressure	increases	...side with fewer moles of gas to reduce the pressure.
	decreases	...side with more moles of gas to increase the pressure.

If concentration of a reagent is changed, the system will respond to reverse the change.

If the concentration of...	The system responds to...
...reactants increases	...make more products.
...reactants decreases	...make more reactants.

Topic 4 — Extracting Metals and Equilibria

Metals and Alloys

Transition Metals

TRANSITION METALS — metals in the centre of the periodic table.

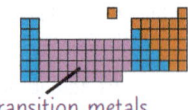

Most metals in the periodic table are transition metals.

Four typical properties of transition metals:

1. High melting points 
2. High densities 
3. Transition metals and their compounds can be good catalysts — e.g. iron in the Haber process.
4. Their ions form colourful compounds. e.g. Fe^{2+} Fe^{3+} Cu^{2+}

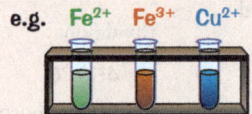

Alloys

ALLOY — a mixture of a metal and at least one other element.

Pure metals are malleable as layers can slide over each other.

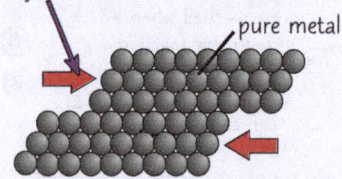
pure metal

New element distorts layers of metal atoms — they can't slide past each other.

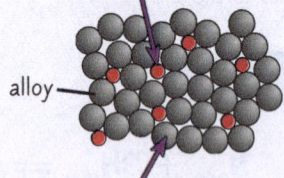
alloy

Alloys are stronger than pure metals.

Uses of Metals and Alloys

Copper

 Malleable and corrosion resistant — used in water pipes.

 Good electrical conductor — used for wiring.

Brass — alloy containing copper and zinc.

 Shiny and strong — used for decorative taps, door fittings.

Steel — alloy containing iron and carbon. Other metals added to make alloy steels.

 Stronger, less likely to rust than iron — used to make long-lasting things, e.g. bridges, saucepans.

Gold

 Good electrical conductor and corrosion resistant — used in electronic components.

 Shiny and malleable — used in jewellery.

 Gold alloys also used for jewellery — gold is strengthened with e.g. zinc, copper, silver.

Aluminium is light and corrosion resistant, but not very strong — used in drinks cans.

Magnalium — alloy containing aluminium and about 5% magnesium. Stronger, lighter and more corrosion resistant than aluminium — used in cars, aeroplanes.

Corrosion

Corrosion and Rusting

CORROSION — damage to metals when they are oxidised by oxygen and water from their environment.

RUSTING — corrosion of iron by water and oxygen (from the air).

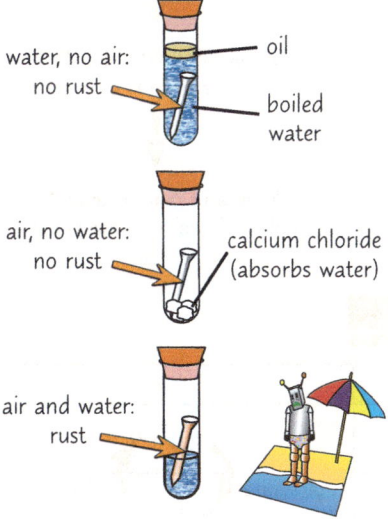

water, no air: no rust — oil / boiled water

air, no water: no rust — calcium chloride (absorbs water)

air and water: rust

Three Ways to Prevent Rusting

1 Barrier methods: coating iron to keep out water and oxygen, e.g. painting, oiling, greasing.

2 Sacrificial protection: attaching a more reactive metal which corrodes first.

3 Galvanisation: type of barrier and sacrificial protection. Iron is coated with a layer of more reactive zinc.

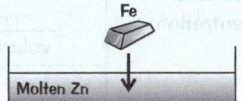

Electroplating

ELECTROPLATING — coating surface of a metal with another metal using electrolysis.

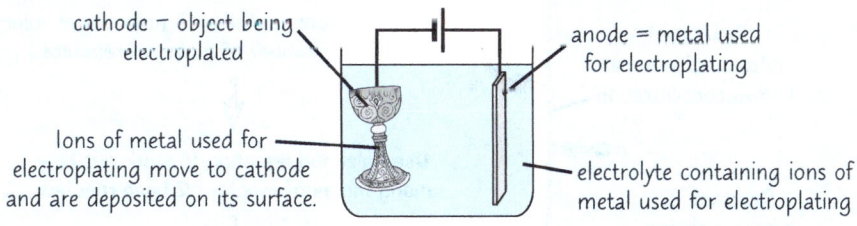

cathode — object being electroplated

anode = metal used for electroplating

Ions of metal used for electroplating move to cathode and are deposited on its surface.

electrolyte containing ions of metal used for electroplating

 Unreactive metals can be coated onto items to prevent corrosion — e.g. for cutlery.

 Precious metals can be coated onto items to improve appearance — e.g. for jewellery.

Topic 5 — Separate Chemistry 1

Gases and Titrations

Molar Volume

MOLAR VOLUME — volume occupied by one mole of gas.

$$\text{molar volume} = \frac{\text{volume of gas}}{\text{number of moles}}$$

AVOGADRO'S LAW — under same conditions, all gases have same molar volume.

At room temperature and pressure (RTP), molar volume of any gas = 24 dm³ mol⁻¹.

RTP = 20 °C and 1 atm

You'll be given this value if you need to use it.

Calculations With Gases

Use balanced equations and mass of solid used up in a reaction to work out volume of gas produced:

Use mass and A_r/M_r of solid to work out number of moles of solid.

⬇

Use balanced equation to find number of moles of gas.

⬇

Volume of gas produced = moles of gas × molar volume.

Calculating Concentration from Titrations

Two ways to calculate concentration:

Concentration = ...	Units
$\dfrac{\text{mass of solute}}{\text{volume of solution}}$	g dm⁻³
$\dfrac{\text{number of moles of solute}}{\text{volume of solution}}$	mol dm⁻³

÷ M_r of solute × M_r of solute

TITRATION — method to find the volume of acid needed to neutralise a given amount of alkali (or vice versa).

Use results of a titration to calculate concentration of an acid or alkali:

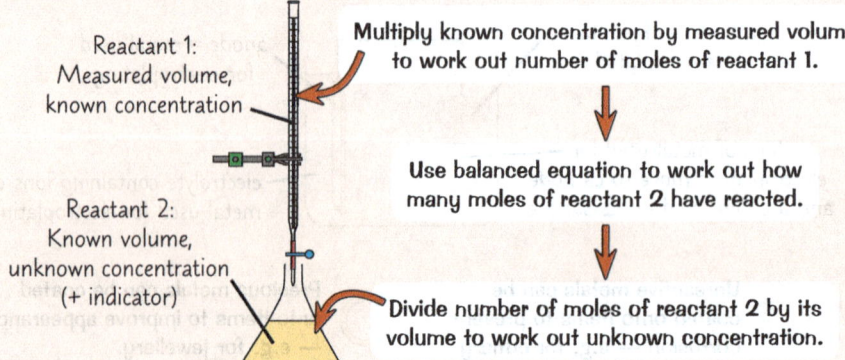

Reactant 1: Measured volume, known concentration

Multiply known concentration by measured volume to work out number of moles of reactant 1.

⬇

Reactant 2: Known volume, unknown concentration (+ indicator)

Use balanced equation to work out how many moles of reactant 2 have reacted.

⬇

Divide number of moles of reactant 2 by its volume to work out unknown concentration.

Percentage Yield and Atom Economy

Percentage Yield

YIELD — the amount of product made in a reaction.

PERCENTAGE YIELD — how much product you get (actual yield) compared to how much you'd get if all reactants converted to products (theoretical yield).

$$\text{Percentage yield} = \frac{\text{actual yield}}{\text{theoretical yield}} \times 100$$

HIGHER % yield = LESS waste of reactants + LOWER costs

Factors Affecting the Yield

Percentage yields are usually lower than 100%.

Three common reasons for this:

1. Incomplete reaction — not all reactants converted.

2. Practical losses — e.g. when transferring product between containers.

3. Unwanted reactions — reactants don't make intended product.

Atom Economy

ATOM ECONOMY — the percentage of the molecular mass of reactants that gets converted into desired products.

$$\text{Atom economy} = \frac{\text{total } M_r \text{ of desired products}}{\text{total } M_r \text{ of all products}} \times 100$$

Three advantages of using reactions with higher atom economies:

1. Use up resources at a slower rate.

2. Don't produce a lot of waste.

3. More profitable.

When choosing a reaction pathway, the yield, rate, equilibrium position, atom economy and usefulness of by-products are all considered.

This means they are more sustainable.

Topic 5 — Separate Chemistry 1

The Haber Process

Producing Ammonia

Exothermic reaction

$N_{2(g)} + 3H_{2(g)} \rightleftharpoons 2NH_{3(g)}$
nitrogen   hydrogen   ammonia

Endothermic reaction

H_2 (extracted from hydrocarbons)

N_2 (from the air)

Hydrogen and nitrogen mixed in 3:1 ratio

This reaction is suited to an industrial scale — the raw materials and the amount of energy needed for the conditions are not too expensive.

450 °C
200 atm

Reaction vessel

Trays of iron catalyst

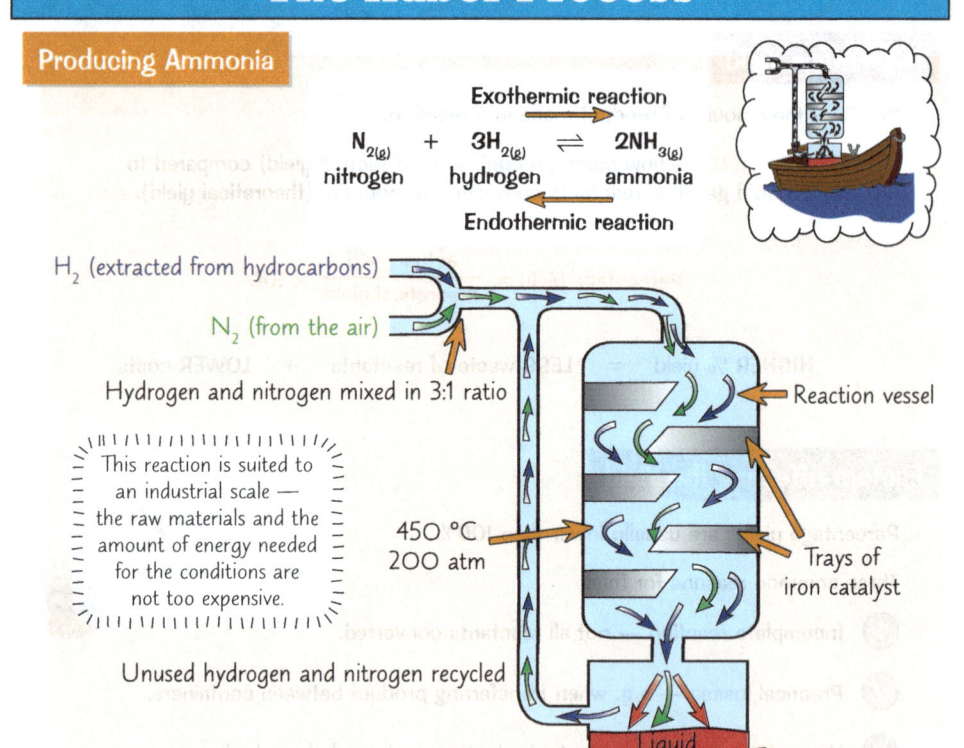

Unused hydrogen and nitrogen recycled

Ammonia removed ← Liquid Ammonia ← Condenser

Reaction Conditions in the Haber Process

	Increase temperature	Increase pressure	Increase reactant concentration	Use a catalyst
Yield	Lower 👎	Higher 👍	Higher 👍	No change
Rate at which equilibrium reached	Faster 👍	Faster 👍	Faster 👍	Faster 👍

Reaction temperature of 450 °C is a compromise between faster rate of reaction and higher yield.

Iron catalyst increases rate of reaction — this means a lower temperature can be used, improving yield without reducing rate.

Pressure is kept as high as possible without becoming dangerous or expensive.

These four factors increase rate at which equilibrium reached for any reversible reaction.

Other industrial processes often have to compromise between yield, rate and cost.

Topic 5 — Separate Chemistry 1

Fertilisers and Fuel Cells

Key Elements in Fertilisers

FERTILISERS — provide extra essential elements to plants to increase crop yields, by making them grow faster and bigger.

The main essential elements in fertilisers are nitrogen, phosphorus and potassium.

Plants need these elements to grow properly.

Ammonia Fertilisers

Ammonia can be reacted with oxygen and water to produce nitric acid.

More ammonia can then be reacted with nitric acid to make ammonium nitrate — a fertiliser:

$$NH_{3(aq)} + HNO_{3(aq)} \rightarrow NH_4NO_{3(aq)}$$

Producing Ammonium Sulfate

Ammonium sulfate is another ammonia fertiliser.

Laboratory production:
- burette
- dilute sulfuric acid
- ammonia solution + methyl orange indicator

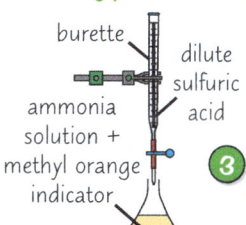

① Do titration to work out exact reaction quantities.

② Mix reactants in exact quantities.

③ Form crystals by gently evaporating solution using steam bath then leaving to cool.

Industrial production:

Not practical to use burettes and steam baths for large quantities.

Several stages required as ammonia and sulfuric acid made from raw materials first.

Fuel Cells

Chemical cells use a chemical reaction to produce a voltage across the cell until one reactant is used up.

FUEL CELL — chemical cell that uses reaction of fuel and oxygen to produce electrical energy.

E.g. hydrogen-oxygen fuel cells produce a voltage. The only waste product is water:
$$2H_2 + O_2 \rightarrow 2H_2O.$$

Evaluating hydrogen-oxygen fuel cells:

Advantages	Disadvantages
Very efficient — electricity generated directly from reaction so fewer places for energy loss.	H_2 difficult to store: • lots of space needed • explosive so must be stored safely
Clean — don't produce greenhouse gases or other pollutants.	H_2 has to be produced from either: • hydrocarbons (non-renewable) • water (uses lots of energy)

Topic 5 — Separate Chemistry 1

Topic 6 — Groups in the Periodic Table

Group 1 and Group 0 Elements

Alkali Metals

ALKALI METALS — common name for Group 1 metals.

Group 1 elements all have one electron in their outer shell.

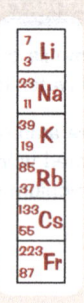

$^{7}_{3}$Li	
$^{23}_{11}$Na	
$^{39}_{19}$K	
$^{85}_{37}$Rb	
$^{133}_{55}$Cs	
$^{223}_{87}$Fr	

Properties of Group 1 Metals

Group 1 metals have different properties from most other metals:

- They're much more reactive.
- They're softer.
- They have lower melting and boiling points.

Reactivity of Group 1 Elements

Readily lose single outer electron to form stable 1+ ion.

Reactivity increases down Group 1 as outer electron is further from nucleus and more easily lost.

Alkali metals react vigorously with water to make alkalis:

alkali metal + water → metal hydroxide + hydrogen

e.g. sodium + water → sodium hydroxide + hydrogen

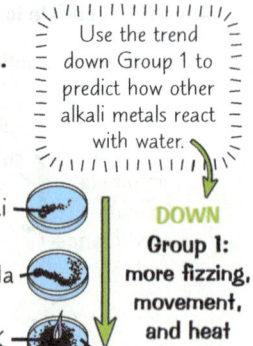

Use the trend down Group 1 to predict how other alkali metals react with water.

DOWN Group 1: more fizzing, movement, and heat

Group 0 Elements

GROUP 0 ELEMENTS — non-metals with full outer shells of electrons.

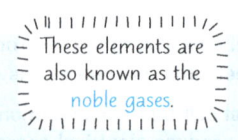

These elements are also known as the noble gases.

Full outer shells are very stable, so these elements are inert (unreactive).

All Group 0 elements are colourless monatomic gases at room temperature.

As you go DOWN Group 0:	
Density	increases
Melting and boiling points	increase

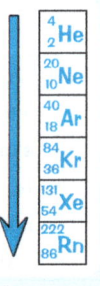

$^{4}_{2}$He	
$^{20}_{10}$Ne	
$^{40}_{18}$Ar	
$^{84}_{36}$Kr	
$^{131}_{54}$Xe	
$^{222}_{86}$Rn	

Property	Uses
Inert	Protect metals during welding
Non-flammable	Filament lamps, flash photography
Low density (just helium)	Fill balloons, airships

Group 7 Elements

Halogens

HALOGENS — the non-metal elements in Group 7.

Halogen	Appearance at room temperature
Chlorine	green gas
Bromine	red-brown liquid which gives off orange vapour
Iodine	dark grey solid which gives off purple vapour

The halogens exist as diatomic molecules — two atoms joined by a covalent bond.

Chlorine gas turns damp blue litmus paper white.

Different states at room temperature show melting and boiling points increase down group.

19	F
9	
35.5	Cl
17	
80	Br
35	
127	I
53	
210	At
85	

Reactions of Group 7 Elements

Halogens have seven outer shell electrons — they gain one electron to form a stable 1− ion.

Reactivity decreases down Group 7 as outer shell is further from nucleus so it's harder to gain an electron.

Hydrogen halides form acidic solutions (e.g. hydrochloric acid) when dissolved in water.

metal + halogen → metal halide

e.g. sodium + chlorine → sodium chloride

hydrogen + halogen → hydrogen halide

e.g. hydrogen + chlorine → hydrogen chloride

Halogen Displacement Reactions

Displacement reactions are redox reactions.

Start with	$KCl_{(aq)}$ (colourless)	$KBr_{(aq)}$ (colourless)	$KI_{(aq)}$ (colourless)
add $Cl_{2(aq)}$ (colourless)	no reaction	orange solution (Br_2)	brown solution (I_2)
add $Br_{2(aq)}$ (orange)	no reaction	no reaction	brown solution (I_2)
add $I_{2(aq)}$ (brown)	no reaction	no reaction	no reaction

Chlorine displaces bromine from an aqueous salt.

$$Cl_{2(aq)} + 2KBr_{(aq)} \rightarrow Br_{2(aq)} + 2KCl_{(aq)}$$

chlorine gains electrons (reduction)

bromide ions lose electrons (oxidation)

Results of displacement reactions show reactivity decreases down Group 7. You'd predict astatine wouldn't displace other halogens as it's at the bottom of Group 7.

Topic 6 — Groups in the Periodic Table

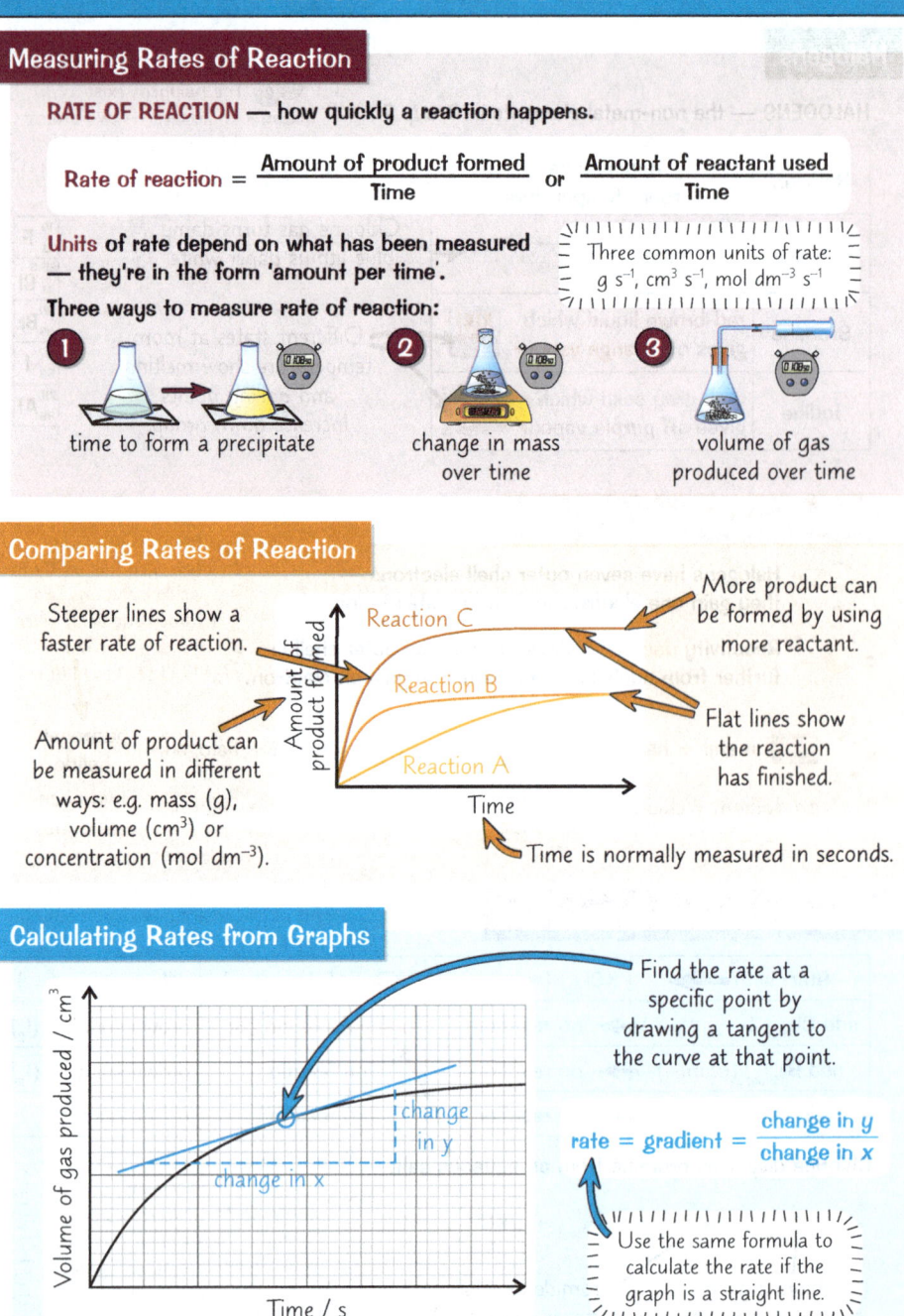

Rates of Reaction

Measuring Rates of Reaction

RATE OF REACTION — how quickly a reaction happens.

$$\text{Rate of reaction} = \frac{\text{Amount of product formed}}{\text{Time}} \text{ or } \frac{\text{Amount of reactant used}}{\text{Time}}$$

Units of rate depend on what has been measured — they're in the form 'amount per time'.

Three common units of rate: $g\ s^{-1}$, $cm^3\ s^{-1}$, $mol\ dm^{-3}\ s^{-1}$

Three ways to measure rate of reaction:

1. time to form a precipitate
2. change in mass over time
3. volume of gas produced over time

Comparing Rates of Reaction

Steeper lines show a faster rate of reaction.

Amount of product can be measured in different ways: e.g. mass (g), volume (cm^3) or concentration ($mol\ dm^{-3}$).

More product can be formed by using more reactant.

Flat lines show the reaction has finished.

Time is normally measured in seconds.

(Graph: Amount of product formed vs Time, showing Reaction C, Reaction B, Reaction A)

Calculating Rates from Graphs

Find the rate at a specific point by drawing a tangent to the curve at that point.

$$\text{rate} = \text{gradient} = \frac{\text{change in } y}{\text{change in } x}$$

Use the same formula to calculate the rate if the graph is a straight line.

(Graph: Volume of gas produced / cm^3 vs Time / s, with tangent showing change in y and change in x)

Factors Affecting Rates of Reaction

Collision Theory

Reactions happen if particles collide with enough energy.

ACTIVATION ENERGY — minimum amount of energy that particles need to react.

Rate depends on...
Collision frequency — the more collisions between particles, the faster the rate of reaction.
Collision energy — the more collisions with at least the activation energy, the faster the rate of reaction.

High energy
High frequency
Fast reaction

Low energy
Low frequency
Slow reaction

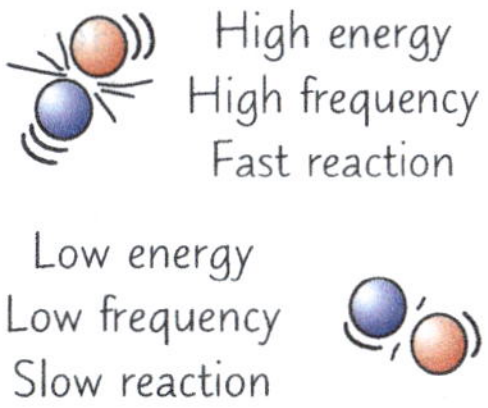

Temperature

Particles move faster and collide more frequently with more energy.

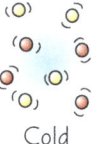

SLOW RATE   FAST RATE
Cold   Hot

Pressure or Concentration

More particles in the same volume — more frequent collisions.

SLOW RATE   FAST RATE
Low pressure/   High pressure/
concentration   concentration

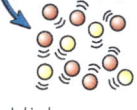

Lower concentration = slower rate of revision

Surface Area

More area for particles to collide with — more frequent collisions.

SLOW RATE   FAST RATE
Big pieces   Small pieces

The smaller the piece of solid, the larger the surface area to volume ratio.

Catalysts

CATALYST — speeds up a reaction without being chemically changed or used up in the reaction, and without changing the products.

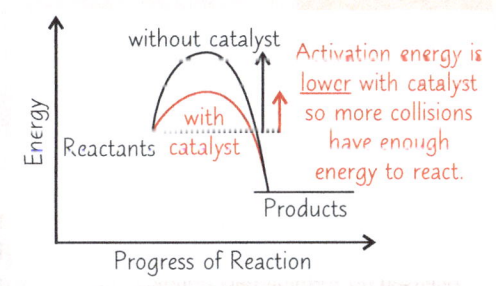

without catalyst
with catalyst
Reactants
Products
Energy
Progress of Reaction

Activation energy is lower with catalyst so more collisions have enough energy to react.

Enzymes are biological catalysts. They can be used to make alcoholic drinks.

Topic 7 — Rates of Reaction and Energy Changes

Endothermic & Exothermic Reactions

Energy Transfer

ENDOTHERMIC REACTION — takes in heat energy from the surroundings (shown by a fall in temperature).

EXOTHERMIC REACTION — gives out heat energy to the surroundings (shown by a rise in temperature).

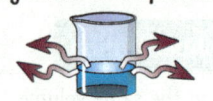

Measuring Temperature Change

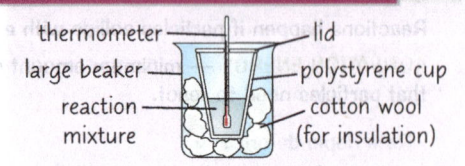

- thermometer
- lid
- large beaker
- polystyrene cup
- reaction mixture
- cotton wool (for insulation)

Record initial temperature and maximum/minimum temperature reached, then calculate temperature change.

You can use this method to investigate:
- dissolving salts in water
- neutralisation, displacement and precipitation reactions.

Reaction Profiles

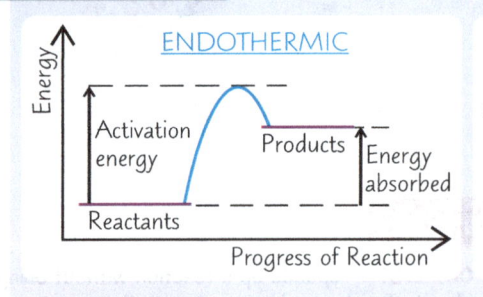

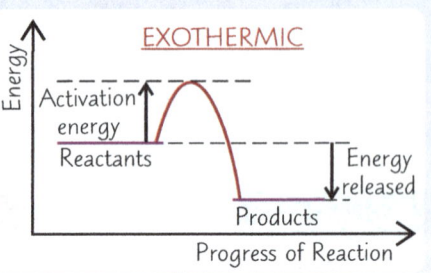

ENDOTHERMIC
- Activation energy
- Reactants
- Products
- Energy absorbed
- Progress of Reaction

EXOTHERMIC
- Activation energy
- Reactants
- Products
- Energy released
- Progress of Reaction

Bond Energies

BOND BREAKING — ENDOTHERMIC

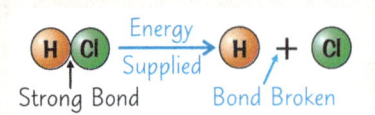

H—Cl + Energy Supplied → H + Cl
Strong Bond / Bond Broken

BOND FORMING — EXOTHERMIC

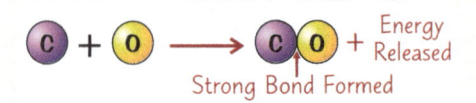

C + O → C—O + Energy Released
Strong Bond Formed

Endothermic reactions: energy used to break bonds is greater than energy released by forming new bonds.

Exothermic reactions: energy released by forming bonds is greater than energy used to break existing bonds.

overall energy change = total energy needed to break bonds − total energy released by forming new bonds

These energies can be calculated from bond energies.

Topic 7 — Rates of Reaction and Energy Changes

Topic 8 — Fuels and Earth Science

Hydrocarbons

Crude Oil

CRUDE OIL — a complex mixture of lots of different hydrocarbons (mostly alkanes).

It's a finite resource.

Hydrocarbons only contain hydrogen and carbon atoms.

Used as a feedstock to create useful substances in petrochemical industry.

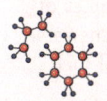

The hydrocarbons have carbon atoms arranged in chains or rings.

Properties of Hydrocarbons

The longer the hydrocarbon chain, the stronger the intermolecular forces — this affects physical properties.

As length of chain increases...	
	...boiling point increases.
	...viscosity increases.
	...ease of ignition decreases.

Hydrocarbons with longer chains contain more C and H atoms. Each crude oil fraction contains hydrocarbons with similar numbers of C and H atoms.

Combustion

COMPLETE COMBUSTION — a reaction that occurs when a fuel reacts with plenty of oxygen.

hydrocarbon + oxygen ⟶ carbon dioxide + water

Hydrocarbons are used as fuels because combustion releases a lot of energy.

Homologous Series

HOMOLOGOUS SERIES — a family of molecules which have the same general formula and share similar chemical properties.

Alkanes are an example of a homologous series.

In a homologous series:

Molecular formulas of neighbouring compounds differ by a CH_2 unit.

Physical properties vary gradually with length of molecule.

Fractional Distillation and Cracking

Fractional Distillation

FRACTIONAL DISTILLATION — a process used to separate the hydrocarbons in crude oil into fractions according to their boiling points. Each fraction has different uses.

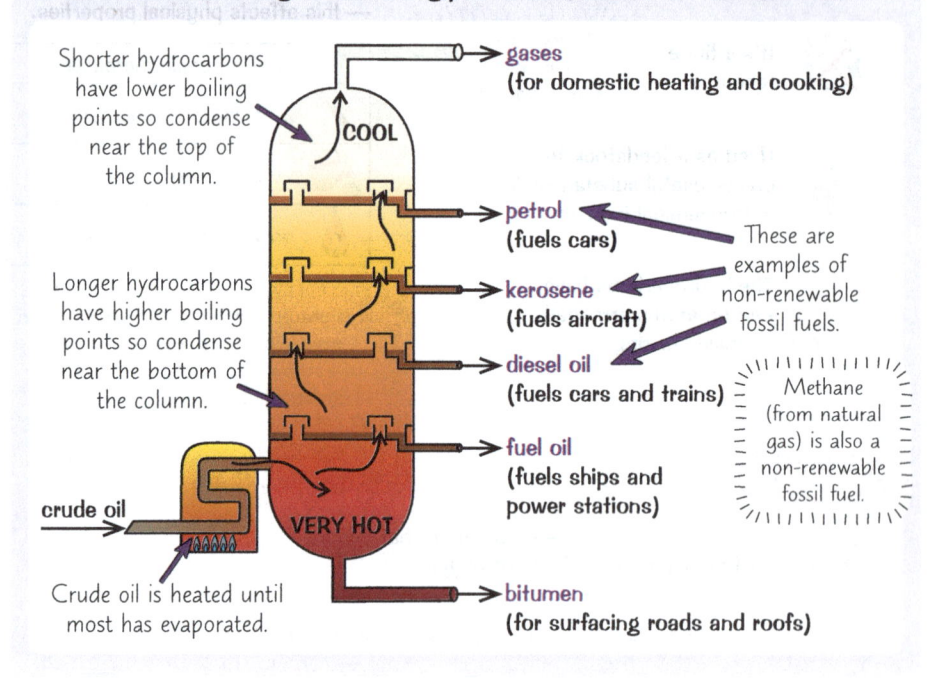

Shorter hydrocarbons have lower boiling points so condense near the top of the column.

COOL

→ gases (for domestic heating and cooking)

→ petrol (fuels cars)

→ kerosene (fuels aircraft)

These are examples of non-renewable fossil fuels.

Longer hydrocarbons have higher boiling points so condense near the bottom of the column.

→ diesel oil (fuels cars and trains)

→ fuel oil (fuels ships and power stations)

Methane (from natural gas) is also a non-renewable fossil fuel.

crude oil →

VERY HOT

Crude oil is heated until most has evaporated.

→ bitumen (for surfacing roads and roofs)

Cracking

There is a high demand for fuels with shorter carbon chains.

CRACKING — breaks down long-chain, saturated hydrocarbons (alkanes) into shorter, more useful molecules.

Alkenes are used to make polymers (mostly plastics).

long-chain alkane ⟹ shorter-chain alkane + unsaturated alkene

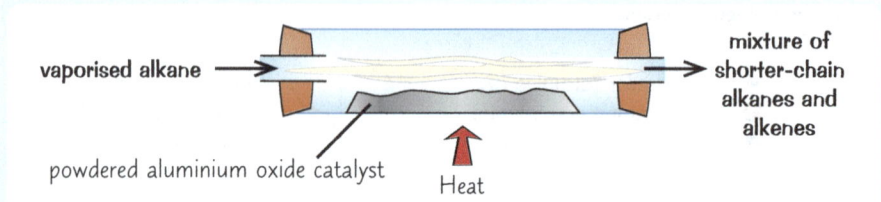

vaporised alkane →

→ mixture of shorter-chain alkanes and alkenes

powdered aluminium oxide catalyst

Heat

Topic 8 — Fuels and Earth Science

Pollutants and Fuels

Air Pollution

Fossil fuels contain hydrocarbons and sometimes sulfur impurities.

Combustion of these fuels releases gases and particles which pollute the air. ← This can happen in appliances that are powered by fossil fuels.

Pollutant	Formation	Effects
Carbon monoxide	carbon monoxide, carbon (soot), water vapour, carbon dioxide	Stops blood from transporting enough oxygen around the body — this can cause fainting, coma or death.
Carbon (soot)	Incomplete combustion of hydrocarbons (occurs when there isn't enough oxygen for complete combustion).	Causes respiratory problems. Reduces air quality. Makes buildings look dirty.
Sulfur dioxide	From sulfur impurities in fossil fuels that react during combustion.	Acid rain — oxides mix with clouds to form acids (NO_x, SO_2)
Oxides of nitrogen	Reaction between nitrogen and oxygen in the air caused by the heat of burning fuels, e.g. in car engines.	damage to trees, statues and buildings. lakes become acidic — plants and animals die

Hydrogen as a Fuel for Vehicles

Advantages	Disadvantages
Very clean — only waste product is water.	Need a special, expensive engine.
Obtained from a renewable resource (water), so won't run out.	Manufacturing hydrogen is expensive, and often uses energy from fossil fuels.
Can be obtained from the water produced by the cell when used in fuel cells.	Hard to store.

Topic 8 — Fuels and Earth Science

The Atmosphere

Volcanic Gases

Intense volcanic activity released gases.

H_2O, NH_3, CH_4, CO_2, CO_2

Early atmosphere probably contained mainly carbon dioxide with some water vapour and small amounts of other gases.

The early atmosphere contained virtually no oxygen gas.

Absorption of Carbon Dioxide

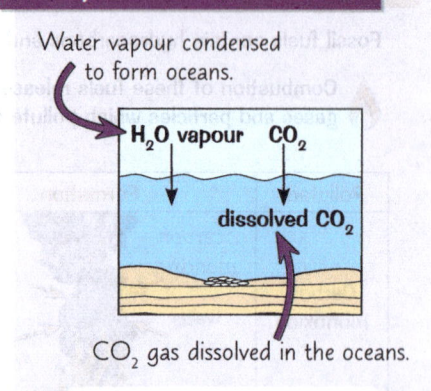

Water vapour condensed to form oceans.

H_2O vapour CO_2

dissolved CO_2

CO_2 gas dissolved in the oceans.

This caused an overall decrease in atmospheric CO_2.

Increase in Oxygen

When green plants evolved, they began to photosynthesise.

Photosynthesis:

Removes carbon dioxide from the air.

Produces oxygen.

Over time, the amount of O_2 in the air gradually built up, and the amount of CO_2 decreased.

Today's Atmosphere

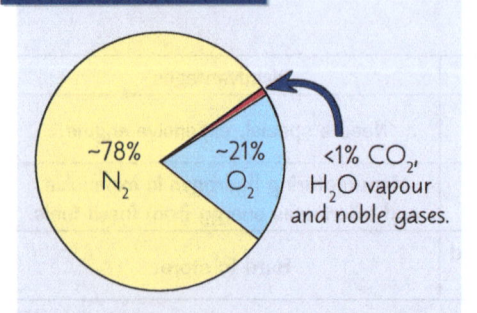

~78% N_2

~21% O_2

<1% CO_2, H_2O vapour and noble gases.

Test for Oxygen Gas

Oxygen will relight a glowing splint.

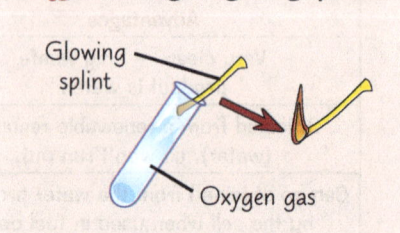

Glowing splint

Oxygen gas

Topic 8 — Fuels and Earth Science

Greenhouse Gases & Climate Change

The Greenhouse Effect

Greenhouse Gases		
carbon dioxide	methane	water vapour

GREENHOUSE EFFECT — when greenhouse gases in the atmosphere absorb long wavelength radiation and re-radiate it in all directions, including back towards Earth, helping to keep the Earth warm.

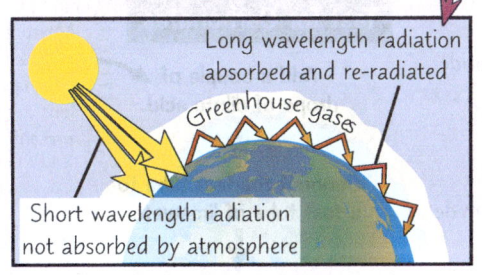

Long wavelength radiation absorbed and re-radiated

Greenhouse gases

Short wavelength radiation not absorbed by atmosphere

Human Activities

Increased population means more greenhouse gases, because more:

Fossil fuels burnt for energy — more CO_2 released.

Deforestation — less CO_2 removed by photosynthesis.

Farming — more methane produced.

There's strong correlation between increased levels of greenhouse gases and global warming.

> Global warming is a type of climate change that can cause other types of climate change.

Climate Change Consequences

Two possible consequences of climate change:

1. Flooding due to the melting of the polar ice caps causing sea levels to rise.
2. Changing rainfall patterns.

Historical Climate Data

- Less accurate and less representative of global levels than modern data.
- Hard to estimate precisely.

Ways of Reducing CO_2 Emissions

Individuals
- Walk/cycle instead of driving.
- Turn down central heating.

Governments
- Use legislation and financial incentives.
- Fund research into new energy sources.

Topic 8 — Fuels and Earth Science

Tests for Ions

Chemical Tests

Tests should be *unique* — it's not useful if different ions give you the same result.

Test for Halides

Add dilute nitric acid followed by silver nitrate solution to mystery solution.

Chloride (Cl⁻) ions give a white precipitate.
— silver chloride

Bromide (Br⁻) ions give a cream precipitate.
— silver bromide

Iodide (I⁻) ions give a yellow precipitate.
— silver iodide

Test for Sulfates

Add dilute hydrochloric acid followed by barium chloride solution to mystery solution.

If *sulfate* (SO_4^{2-}) ions are present, a white precipitate will form.

barium sulfate precipitate

Test for Carbonates

Add a couple of drops of dilute acid.

Mixture will fizz if carbonate ions are present.

↓

Connect the test tube to a test tube of limewater.

↓

Carbonate ions (CO_3^{2-}) react to form carbon dioxide, which will turn the limewater milky.

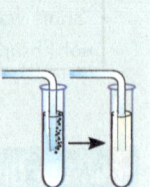

Test for Cations with NaOH

Test for metal cations:

Add a few drops of sodium hydroxide (NaOH) solution to mystery solution.

Metal Ion	Colour of Precipitate
Calcium, Ca^{2+}	White
Copper(II), Cu^{2+}	Blue
Iron(II), Fe^{2+}	Green
Iron(III), Fe^{3+}	Brown
Aluminium, Al^{3+}	White

Redissolves in excess NaOH to form a colourless solution.

Test for ammonium ions:

Add sodium hydroxide solution to mystery solution and gently heat.

If *ammonium* (NH_4^+) ions are present, ammonia gas (NH_3) will be given off.

Ammonia gas turns damp red litmus paper blue.

More Tests and Flame Photometry

Flame Tests for Metal Cations

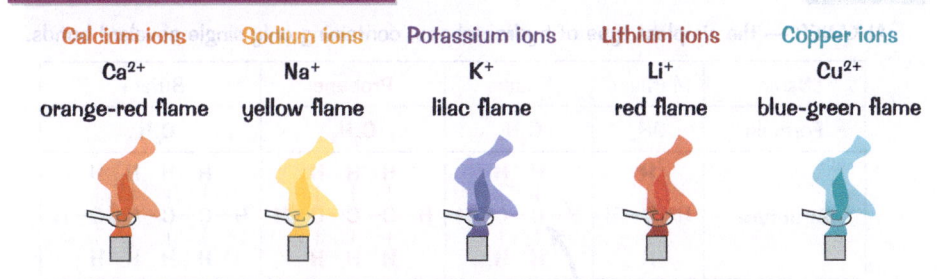

Calcium ions	Sodium ions	Potassium ions	Lithium ions	Copper ions
Ca^{2+}	Na^+	K^+	Li^+	Cu^{2+}
orange-red flame	yellow flame	lilac flame	red flame	blue-green flame

Disadvantage of flame tests — if the sample contains a mixture of metal ions, the flame colours of some ions may be hidden by the colours of others.

Three Advantages of Instrumental Analysis

INSTRUMENTAL ANALYSIS — tests that use machines.

1) Sensitive — can detect even the tiniest amounts

2) Fast — tests can be automated

3) Accurate — don't involve human error

"Hmm... Maybe potassium?"

Two Uses of Flame Photometry

Flame photometry is an example of instrumental analysis.

1) Identifying ions in solution — each ion produces a unique line spectrum so you can compare with reference spectra.

If multiple ions are present in a sample, the spectrum will be a combination of all their individual spectra.

2) Determining the concentration of ions — this can be calculated from the intensity of the lines on the spectrum.

Read from the curve to find concentration that corresponds to measured intensity.

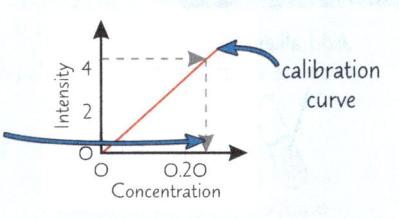

calibration curve

Topic 9 — Separate Chemistry 2

Types of Hydrocarbons

Alkanes

ALKANES — the simplest type of hydrocarbons, containing only single covalent bonds.

Name	Methane	Ethane	Propane	Butane
Formula	CH_4	C_2H_6	C_3H_8	C_4H_{10}
Structure	H–C(H)(H)–H	H–C(H)(H)–C(H)(H)–H	H–C(H)(H)–C(H)(H)–C(H)(H)–H	H–C(H)(H)–C(H)(H)–C(H)(H)–C(H)(H)–H

All atoms have formed single covalent bonds with as many other atoms as possible — alkanes are saturated.

Alkenes

ALKENES — hydrocarbons that have one C=C double bond functional group.

Functional group — a group of atoms in a molecule that dictate how that molecule typically reacts.

Name	Ethene	Propene	But-1-ene	But-2-ene
Formula	C_2H_4	C_3H_6	C_4H_8	C_4H_8
Structure	H₂C=CH₂	H–C(H)(H)–C(H)=CH₂	H–C(H)(H)–C(H)(H)–C(H)=CH₂	H–C(H)(H)–C(H)=C(H)–C(H)(H)–H

Alkenes are unsaturated — double bond can open up to form other bonds.

Alkenes can undergo addition reactions where another substance adds across the C=C double bond, e.g. ethene reacts with bromine:

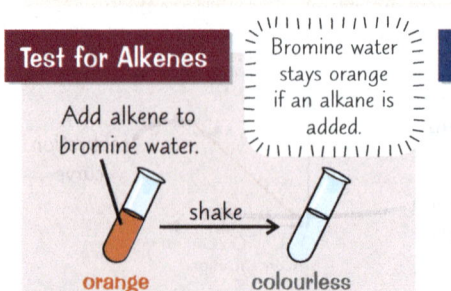

$$H_2C=CH_2 + Br_2 \rightarrow H_2C(Br)-C(Br)H_2$$

Test for Alkenes

Add alkene to bromine water.

Bromine water stays orange if an alkane is added.

shake → orange becomes colourless

Combustion

Alkanes and alkenes burn in oxygen.

Hydrocarbons are oxidised during complete combustion:

hydrocarbon + oxygen → carbon dioxide + water

Topic 9 — Separate Chemistry 2

Addition Polymers

Addition Polymerisation

POLYMERS — substances made by joining lots of small repeating units. They have a high average M_r.

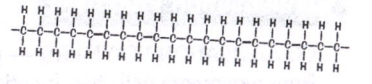

ADDITION POLYMERISATION — when molecules with C=C bonds join together in addition reactions.

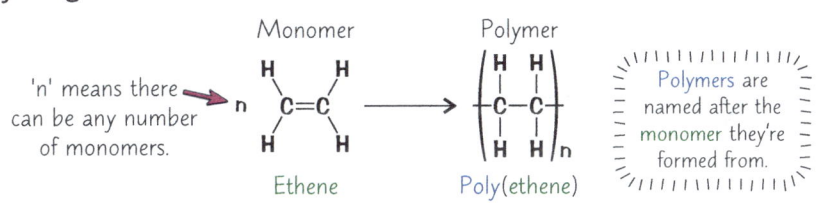

'n' means there can be any number of monomers.

Monomer: Ethene

Polymer: Poly(ethene)

Polymers are named after the monomer they're formed from.

Other addition polymers form in the same way — double bonds open up to join monomers together.

Drawing Polymers

Four steps for drawing the displayed formula of a polymer from its monomer:

propene → poly(propene)

To draw the monomer from the polymer, just reverse the method below.

① Draw the alkene carbons and replace the double bond with a single bond.

② Add an extra single bond to each carbon atom.

③ Add the other groups in the same way that they surrounded the double bond.

④ Add the brackets and 'n'.

Uses of Polymers

	Properties		Uses
Poly(ethene)	flexible, cheap, electrical insulator		carrier bags, wire insulation
Poly(propene)	flexible, strong, tough, mouldable		plastic crates, ropes
Poly(chloroethene) (PVC)	tough, cheap		window frames, water pipes
Poly(tetrafluoroethene) (PTFE)	unreactive, tough, non-stick		non-stick pans, waterproof clothing

Topic 9 — Separate Chemistry 2

More Polymers and Plastics

Condensation Polymers

CONDENSATION POLYMERS — polymers formed from monomers with two functional groups.

In condensation polymerisation, a small molecule is lost for each new bond formed.

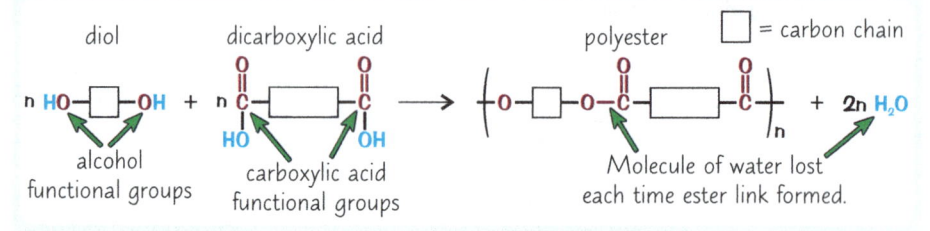

diol + dicarboxylic acid → polyester + $2n\ H_2O$

□ = carbon chain

alcohol functional groups

carboxylic acid functional groups

Molecule of water lost each time ester link formed.

Natural Polymers

DNA — complex molecule that contains genetic information.

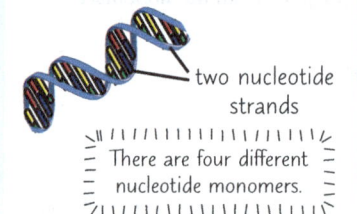

two nucleotide strands

There are four different nucleotide monomers.

STARCH — a polymer made from sugars.

Sugars are small molecules containing carbon, oxygen and hydrogen.

PROTEINS — condensation polymers of amino acids.

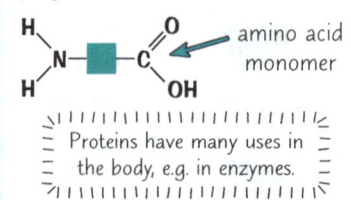

amino acid monomer

Proteins have many uses in the body, e.g. in enzymes.

Recycling Plastics

Advantages

- Less plastics have to be disposed of — this means:
  - less non-biodegradable waste going to landfill
  - less carbon dioxide and toxic gases released by burning plastics.
- Generally uses fewer resources than making new plastics, which are made from crude oil (finite resource).
- Generally saves money and creates jobs.

Disadvantages

- Must be separated before melting down — difficult and expensive.
- Melting down can still release polluting gases.
- Over time, strength of polymer decreases — can't recycle same polymer forever.

Topic 9 — Separate Chemistry 2

Alcohols and Carboxylic Acids

Alcohols

ALCOHOLS — a compound containing an –OH functional group.

Name	Methanol	Ethanol	Propanol	Butanol
Formula	CH_3OH	C_2H_5OH	C_3H_7OH	C_4H_9OH
Structure	H–C–O–H (with H above and below)	H–C–C–O–H	e.g. H–C–C–C–O–H	e.g. H–C–C–C–C–O–H

Make alkenes from alcohols by heating alcohol with acid catalyst. ← This is a dehydration reaction as a molecule of water is lost from the alcohol.

Carboxylic Acids

CARBOXYLIC ACIDS — a compound containing a –COOH functional group.

Carboxylic acid solutions have the same properties as other weak acid solutions.

Name	Methanoic acid	Ethanoic acid	Propanoic acid	Butanoic acid
Formula	HCOOH	CH_3COOH	C_2H_5COOH	C_3H_7COOH
Structure	H–C(=O)–O–H	H–C–C(=O)–O–H	H–C–C–C(=O)–O–H	H–C–C–C–C(=O)–O–H

Carboxylic acids can be made by oxidising alcohols — e.g. ethanol can be oxidised to form ethanoic acid.

Members of a homologous series have similar reactions as they share a functional group.

Fermentation

FERMENTATION — process where a yeast enzyme converts solutions of carbohydrates (e.g. sugar) into alcohol.

Fermentation only produces a dilute solution of ethanol — yeast die when concentration too high.

Fractional distillation is used to concentrate the ethanol solution:

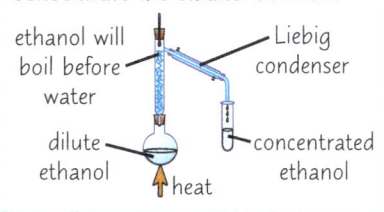

sugar —yeast→ ethanol + carbon dioxide

ethanol will boil before water

dilute ethanol → heat → concentrated ethanol

Liebig condenser

Optimum conditions for fermentation	
30 – 40 °C	Anaerobic conditions

Topic 9 — Separate Chemistry 2

Nanoparticles and Materials

Particle Sizes

	Diameter (nm)
Atoms and simple molecules	0.1 – 1
Nanoparticles	1 – 100

contain a few hundred atoms

surface area to volume ratio = SA ÷ V

Nanoparticles have a high SA to V ratio compared to larger particles — this gives them different properties to bulk materials.

Uses of Nanoparticles

Catalysts — more surface area means faster rate of reaction.

Medicines — small particles could be absorbed right into target cells.

Cosmetics, e.g. sunscreen — small particles provide more protection and don't leave marks on skin.

There is a risk that nanoparticle products could have harmful effects on health. E.g. nanoparticles could build up in cells over time if they don't get broken down.

Materials and their Uses

You can use data about properties of materials to assess their suitability for different uses.

		Properties	Uses
	POLYMERS Many small monomers bonded in long chains.	Thermal and electrical insulators	Electrical casing
		Often flexible, can be moulded	Carrier bags, squeezy bottles
		Lower density than metals, ceramics	
CERAMICS	**Clay** Soft mineral hardened by firing.	Can be moulded/shaped	Bricks
		Strong	Pottery
	Glass E.g. soda-lime glass made by heating limestone, sand and sodium carbonate.	Brittle	Glassware
		Glass is transparent	
	COMPOSITES One material (reinforcement) embedded in another (matrix/binder).	Depend on materials used. E.g. concrete is strong and dense	Buildings
		Carbon fibre is strong and light	Sports cars
	METALS	Thermal and electrical conductors	Wiring
		Malleable	

Topic 9 — Separate Chemistry 2

Core Practicals 1

Two Techniques for Investigating Composition of Inks

1 Simple distillation can separate solvent from dyes if solvent has lowest boiling point:

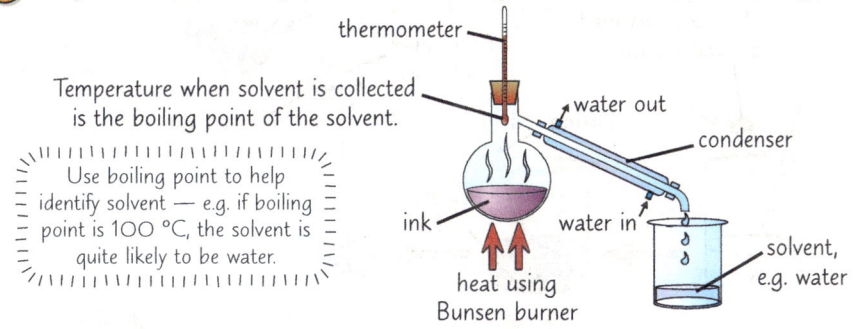

Temperature when solvent is collected is the boiling point of the solvent.

Use boiling point to help identify solvent — e.g. if boiling point is 100 °C, the solvent is quite likely to be water.

Labels: thermometer, water out, condenser, ink, water in, solvent, e.g. water, heat using Bunsen burner

2 Paper chromatography can separate out different dyes:

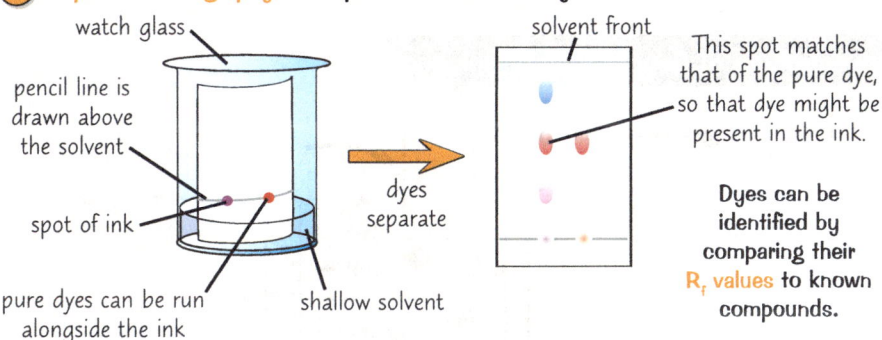

Labels: watch glass, pencil line is drawn above the solvent, spot of ink, pure dyes can be run alongside the ink, shallow solvent, dyes separate, solvent front

This spot matches that of the pure dye, so that dye might be present in the ink.

Dyes can be identified by comparing their R_f values to known compounds.

The experiment should be repeated to see if the spots still match in different solvents.

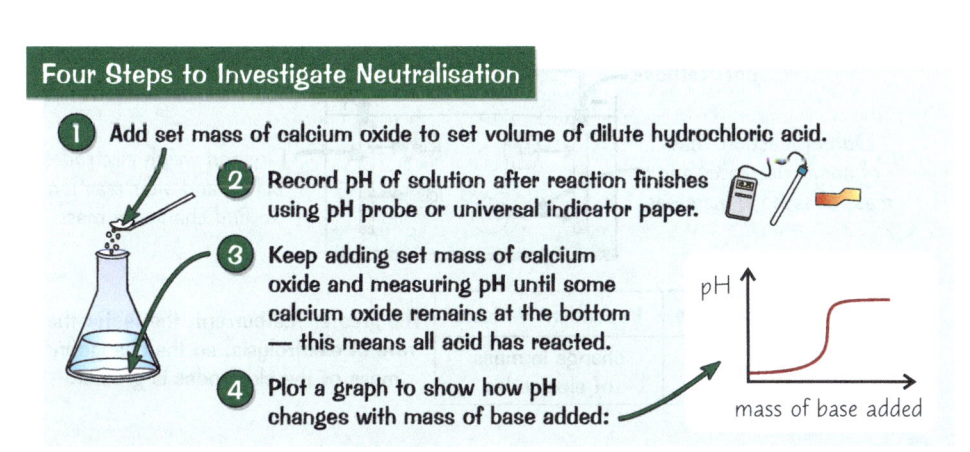

Four Steps to Investigate Neutralisation

1 Add set mass of calcium oxide to set volume of dilute hydrochloric acid.

2 Record pH of solution after reaction finishes using pH probe or universal indicator paper.

3 Keep adding set mass of calcium oxide and measuring pH until some calcium oxide remains at the bottom — this means all acid has reacted.

4 Plot a graph to show how pH changes with mass of base added:

Graph axes: pH vs mass of base added

Core Practicals 2

Making Copper Sulfate

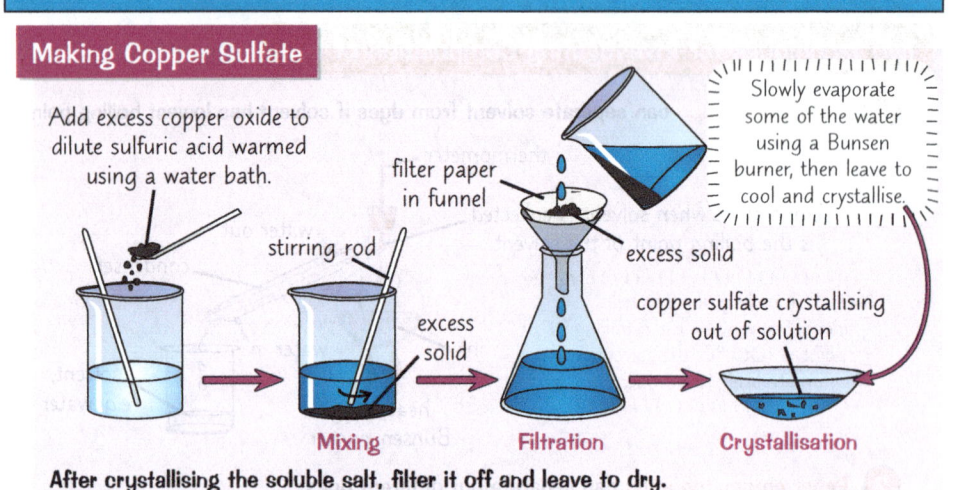

Add excess copper oxide to dilute sulfuric acid warmed using a water bath.

filter paper in funnel

Slowly evaporate some of the water using a Bunsen burner, then leave to cool and crystallise.

stirring rod

excess solid

excess solid

copper sulfate crystallising out of solution

Mixing → **Filtration** → **Crystallisation**

After crystallising the soluble salt, filter it off and leave to dry.

Electrolysis of Copper Sulfate Solution

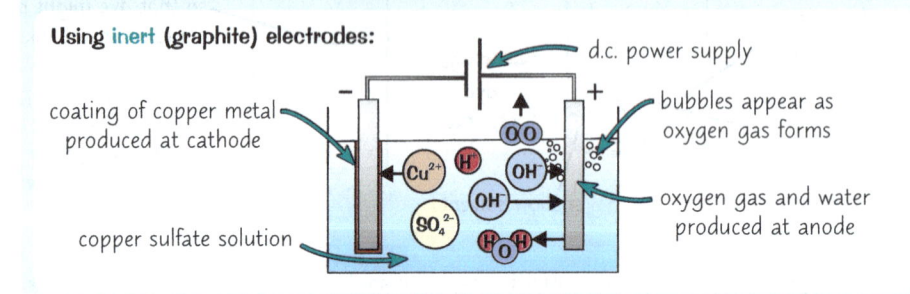

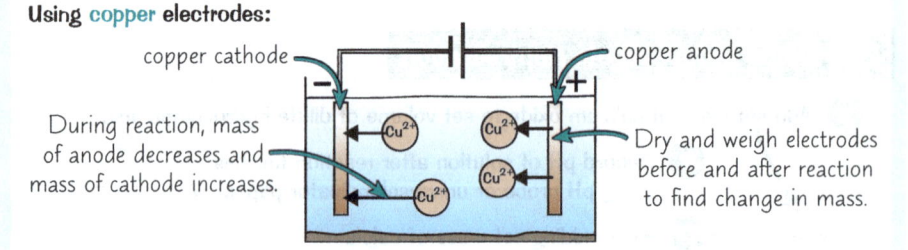

Using inert (graphite) electrodes:

d.c. power supply

coating of copper metal produced at cathode

bubbles appear as oxygen gas forms

oxygen gas and water produced at anode

copper sulfate solution

Ions shown: Cu^{2+}, H^+, OH^-, SO_4^{2-}, H_2O

Using copper electrodes:

copper cathode

copper anode

During reaction, mass of anode decreases and mass of cathode increases.

Dry and weigh electrodes before and after reaction to find change in mass.

Independent Variable	Dependent Variable
current	change in mass of electrodes

The greater the current, the faster the rate of electrolysis, so the change in mass of the electrodes is greater.

Core Practicals

Core Practicals 3

Titrations

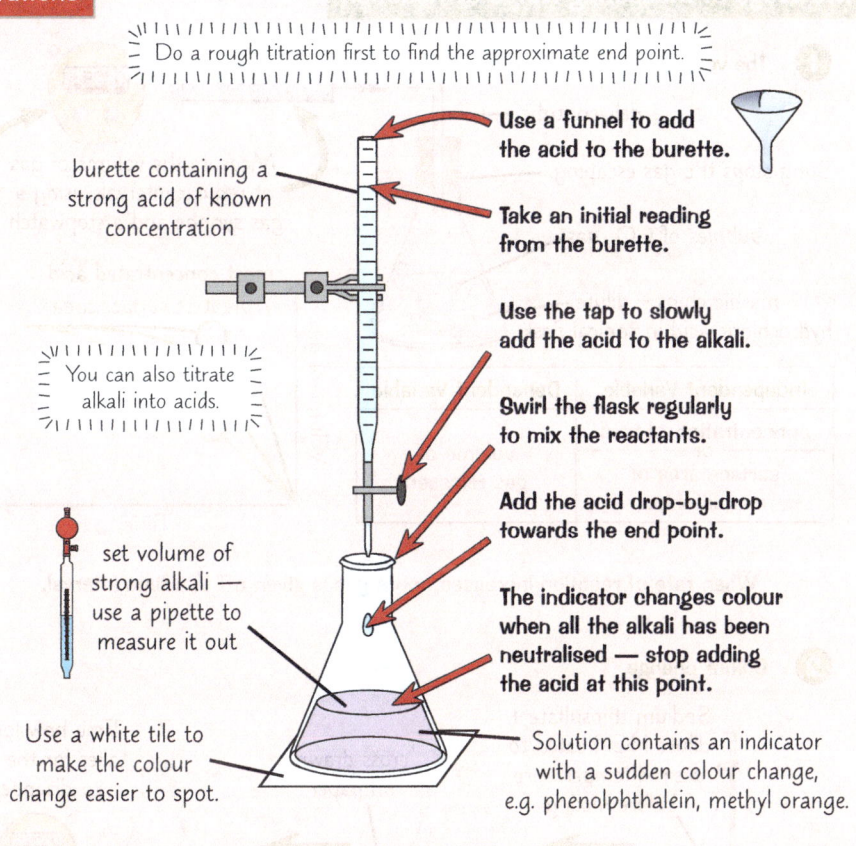

Do a rough titration first to find the approximate end point.

- burette containing a strong acid of known concentration
- Use a funnel to add the acid to the burette.
- Take an initial reading from the burette.
- Use the tap to slowly add the acid to the alkali.
- *You can also titrate alkali into acids.*
- Swirl the flask regularly to mix the reactants.
- Add the acid drop-by-drop towards the end point.
- set volume of strong alkali — use a pipette to measure it out
- The indicator changes colour when all the alkali has been neutralised — stop adding the acid at this point.
- Use a white tile to make the colour change easier to spot.
- Solution contains an indicator with a sudden colour change, e.g. phenolphthalein, methyl orange.

When end point is reached, take another reading from the burette and calculate volume added at end point:

Volume of acid added (titre) = difference between the two readings.

Repeat the titration until you get several similar results, then find the mean titre.

Use mean titre, concentration of acid and volume of alkali to calculate the concentration of the alkali solution.

You also need to know the balanced equation for the reaction.

Safety tip #318: don't play with burettes.

Core Practicals 4

Two Ways of Measuring Rates of Reaction

① The volume of gas given off

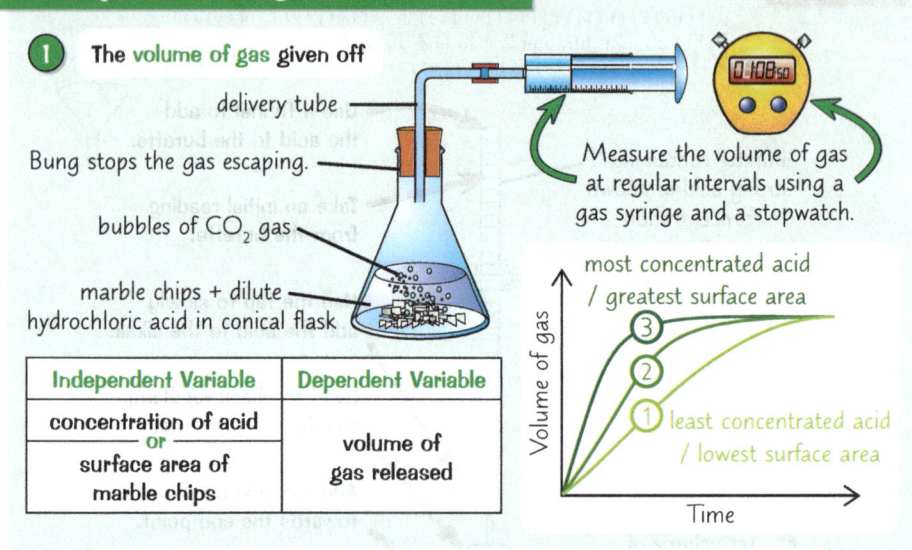

- delivery tube
- Bung stops the gas escaping.
- bubbles of CO_2 gas
- marble chips + dilute hydrochloric acid in conical flask

Measure the volume of gas at regular intervals using a gas syringe and a stopwatch.

Independent Variable	Dependent Variable
concentration of acid — or — surface area of marble chips	volume of gas released

Graph — Volume of gas vs Time:
- ③ most concentrated acid / greatest surface area
- ②
- ① least concentrated acid / lowest surface area

When rate of reaction increases, more gas is given off in a time interval.

② Colour change

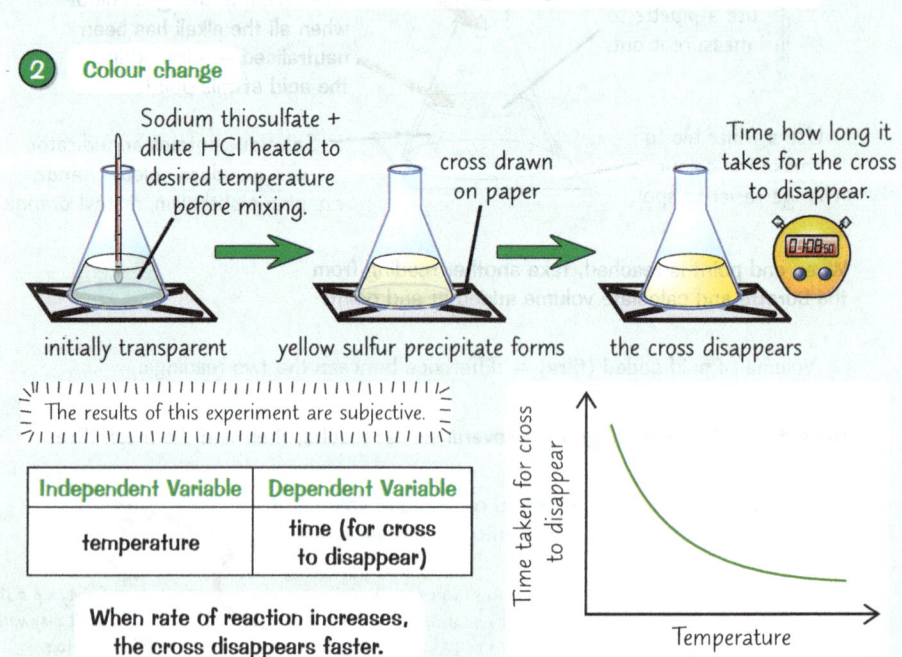

Sodium thiosulfate + dilute HCl heated to desired temperature before mixing. → cross drawn on paper → Time how long it takes for the cross to disappear.

- initially transparent
- yellow sulfur precipitate forms
- the cross disappears

The results of this experiment are subjective.

Independent Variable	Dependent Variable
temperature	time (for cross to disappear)

When rate of reaction increases, the cross disappears faster.

Graph — Time taken for cross to disappear vs Temperature (decreasing curve).

Core Practicals

Core Practicals 5

Identifying Ions

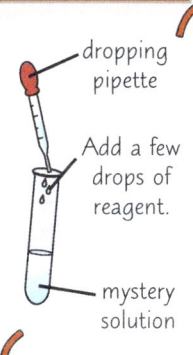

Ion	Test	Observation
Cl⁻	Add dilute nitric acid, then silver nitrate solution.	white precipitate
Br⁻		cream precipitate
I⁻		yellow precipitate
SO_4^{2-}	Add dilute hydrochloric acid, then barium chloride solution.	white precipitate
CO_3^{2-}	Add dilute acid and connect test tube to a test tube of limewater.	limewater turns milky
NH_4^+	Warm with NaOH solution. Test for NH_3 gas with damp red litmus paper.	litmus paper turns blue

- dropping pipette
- Add a few drops of reagent.
- mystery solution

Some metal ions form a coloured precipitate with NaOH solution.

Ca^{2+}	white
Cu^{2+}	blue
Fe^{2+}	green
Fe^{3+}	brown
Al^{3+}	white

Precipitate redissolves in excess NaOH to form a colourless solution.

Three steps for performing flame tests

1. Clean a nichrome wire loop — dip it in hydrochloric acid then rinse with distilled water.
2. Dip the loop into the sample.
3. Hold the loop in a blue Bunsen flame.

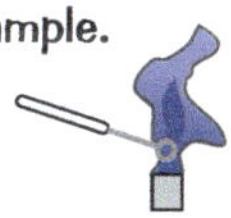

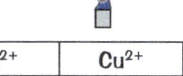

Li^+	Na^+	K^+	Ca^{2+}	Cu^{2+}
red	yellow	lilac	orange-red	blue-green

Combustion of Alcohols

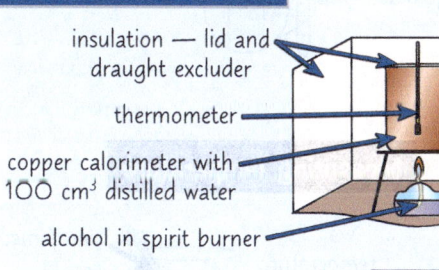

- insulation — lid and draught excluder
- thermometer
- copper calorimeter with 100 cm³ distilled water
- alcohol in spirit burner

1. Measure mass of burner and initial temperature of water.
2. Light the burner — keep lit until temperature of water has increased by 20 °C.
3. Immediately measure mass of burner again to find mass of alcohol used.

Independent Variable	Dependent Variable
type of alcohol	mass of alcohol used

ethanol → propanol → butanol → pentanol

- Carbon chain length increases.
- Mass of fuel used decreases.
- Fuel efficiency increases.

Core Practicals

Apparatus and Techniques

Measuring Mass

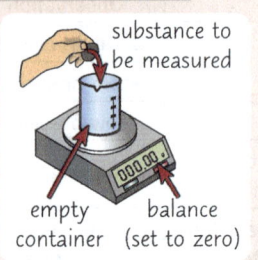

- substance to be measured
- empty container
- balance (set to zero)

Transferring solid to reaction vessel:

When making a solution, wash remaining solid out of the weighing container with the solvent you're dissolving it in.

or

Find the difference in mass of the container and its contents before and after you transfer the solid.

Three Ways to Measure Liquids

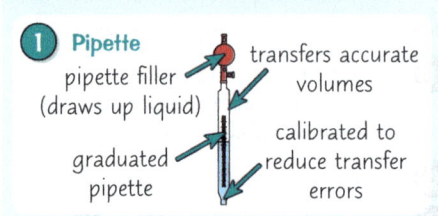

1) Pipette
- pipette filler (draws up liquid)
- graduated pipette
- transfers accurate volumes
- calibrated to reduce transfer errors

2) Burette
- Volume of liquid used is the difference between the initial and final readings on the scale.
- scale measures from top to bottom
- tap releases liquid into a container

3) Measuring cylinder
- Pick a suitable size for volume required.

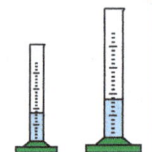

When measuring volumes of liquids: Always read the volume from the bottom of the meniscus. — meniscus

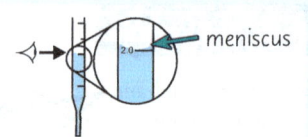

Measuring Time

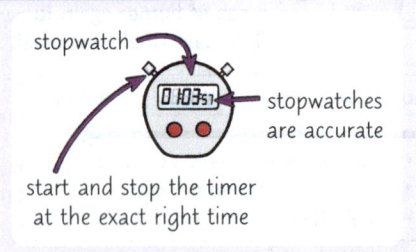

- stopwatch
- stopwatches are accurate
- start and stop the timer at the exact right time

Measuring Temperature

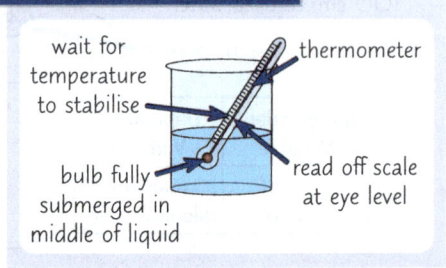

- wait for temperature to stabilise
- thermometer
- bulb fully submerged in middle of liquid
- read off scale at eye level

Practical Skills

Practical Techniques

Measuring pH

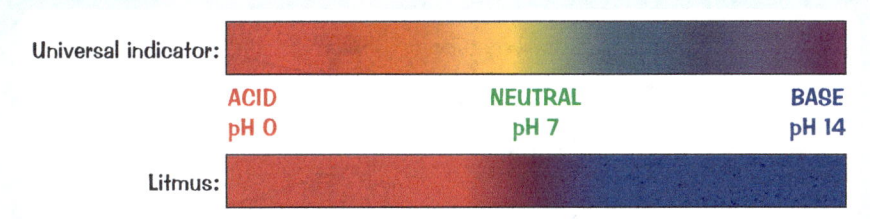

Universal indicator:

| ACID | NEUTRAL | BASE |
| pH 0 | pH 7 | pH 14 |

Litmus:

Indicator solution	Indicator paper
Changes colour of whole solution	For testing a few drops of solution
Good for showing the end point in titrations	Use damp indicator paper to test gases

pH probes and **pH meters** give a numerical value for **pH**.

pH meter
pH probe

Safety Precautions

Read the safety precautions to do with your method before you start any experiment.

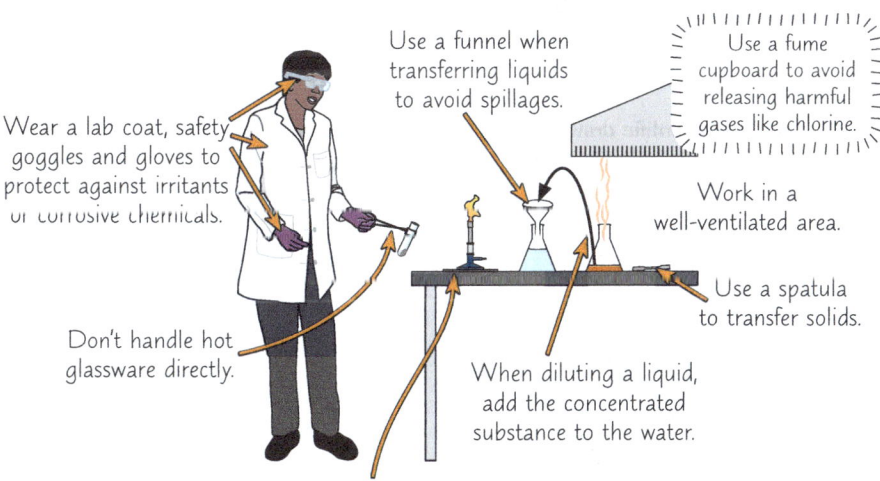

Wear a lab coat, safety goggles and gloves to protect against irritants or corrosive chemicals.

Use a funnel when transferring liquids to avoid spillages.

Use a fume cupboard to avoid releasing harmful gases like chlorine.

Work in a well-ventilated area.

Use a spatula to transfer solids.

Don't handle hot glassware directly.

When diluting a liquid, add the concentrated substance to the water.

Keep heat sources away from flammable chemicals.

Practical Skills

Equipment and Heating Substances

Collecting Gases

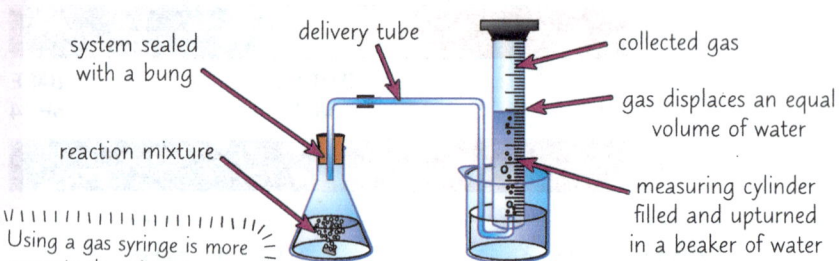

- system sealed with a bung
- delivery tube
- collected gas
- gas displaces an equal volume of water
- reaction mixture
- measuring cylinder filled and upturned in a beaker of water

Using a gas syringe is more accurate than this — some gases dissolve in water which affects the amount in the measuring cylinder.

Amount of gas collected is the difference between the initial and final volumes in the cylinder.

Using Bunsen Burners

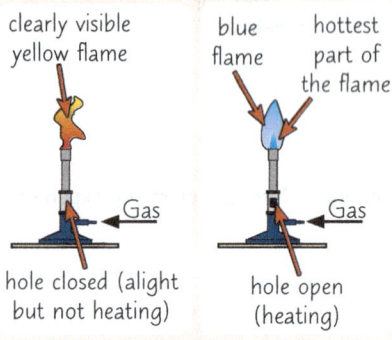

clearly visible yellow flame ← Gas
hole closed (alight but not heating)

blue flame — hottest part of the flame ← Gas
hole open (heating)

You can use scientific drawings to show how apparatus is set up:
- test tube
- beaker
- gauze
- tripod
- Bunsen burner
- heat-proof mat

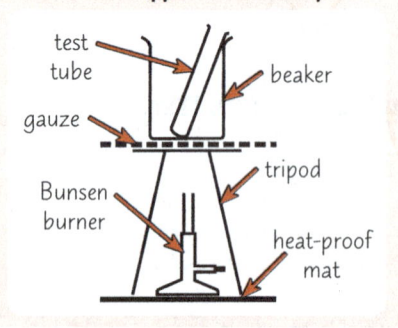

Other Heating Methods

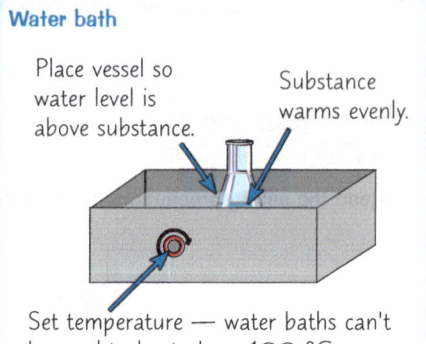

Water bath
Place vessel so water level is above substance. Substance warms evenly.

Set temperature — water baths can't be used to heat above 100 °C.

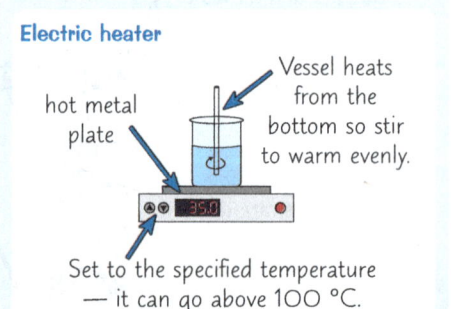

Electric heater
hot metal plate
Vessel heats from the bottom so stir to warm evenly.

Set to the specified temperature — it can go above 100 °C.

Yay! You've only gone and made it through ALL the facts. Give yourself a round of applause.

Practical Skills